425.

THE
HIGH CHURCH
SCHISM

First published, October, 1951

PRINTED IN GREAT BRITAIN
in 10pt. Baskerville type
BY THE FAITH PRESS, LTD.
LEIGHTON BUZZARD

THE HIGH CHURCH SCHISM

FOUR LECTURES ON THE NONJURORS

BY

J. W. C. WAND
Bishop of London

LONDON
THE FAITH PRESS, LTD.
7 TUFTON STREET, WESTMINSTER, S.W. I
MOREHOUSE - GORHAM CO., NEW YORK, U.S.A.

PREFACE

By special request our Lent Lectures this year were to deal with a topic of *modern* Church history. I chose the story of the Nonjurors, both as being of immense interest in itself, and also as offering suggestions of special value in our frustrated and divided age.

I have to thank Mr. R. H. Collier, who has himself just completed a life of Hickes, not only for giving me the benefit of his special researches, but also for very kindly reading my proofs.

W.L.

v

CONTENTS

CHAPTER I

THE ORIGIN OF THE SCHISM

I

IT is the present fashion in historical writing to concentrate upon the life of the people and to ignore, as far as possible, kings and all those in authority. This is perhaps in accord with political trends, and for the time at least it has the attraction of novelty. It may be doubted, however, whether it is entirely realistic. No doubt our main interest lies in knowing how people like ourselves lived in the past. It would, however, be fantastic to write as though there was no vital association between the fate of kings and the welfare of their subjects. In some cases indeed the fortunes of the one are wrapped up indissolubly with the fate of the other.

In no instance is this more true than in the case of the Nonjurors. The temporal fortunes of these people were entirely dependent upon those of the person whom they deemed their king. It might be possible for us to say that they were so small a section of the community that their vicissitudes were not then of general interest and are not of much concern to us to-day. That would be to misunderstand the conditions of their time and to underestimate the influence they exercised upon their own and subsequent generations. Their king cost them all they had. They lost him his throne and might easily have become the cause of his restoration.

Their influence may still be seen in the prevailing doctrinal emphasis within the Church of England and indeed throughout the Anglican Communion, to say nothing of other sections of Christendom. Certainly it would be true to say that in the Anglican Communion itself the influence of the Nonjurors is still felt in the details of public worship and particularly in the method of celebrating the Eucharist. A more general question, the discussion of which was forced upon them by the peculiar conditions of their time and which has its interest to-day not only for the ecclesiastical historian but also for the statesman and constitutional lawyer, is that of the relation between Church and State. A special interest in this question is being shown in our own country at the present time because of the problems of Church reform and the necessity of determining what part the State shall play in them. That this interest is not confined to our own country and to the peculiar position of an Established Church is shown by every newspaper which brings us fresh news of difficulties in the relation between secular and ecclesiastical authorities on the Continent. There the churches are compelled to give anguished consideration to the best attitude to adopt towards the encroachments of tyrannical and unsympathetic governments. If this is not enough to show the continued importance of the Nonjurors in our own time, we may further instance the need to resolve a very personal problem which has a particular importance in every country where monarchy prevails. In what sense are we to interpret the oath of allegiance to a reigning monarch? If we have been able to arrive at a satisfactory answer to that question, it is very largely because of the intense consideration that was given to it in this country at the end of the seventeenth century.

II

Although the Nonjuring Schism was a purely domestic affair, the course of circumstances which gave rise to it and kept it in being for a century or so was inevitably influenced by events outside this country. It was the period when Louis XIV was endeavouring to extend his power, and was consequently at feud both with the Pope and with the Emperor. Not only so, but Christendom itself was fighting for existence against the Turk, who was compelled to relinquish Belgrade in 1688, but returned to the attack later. Peter the Great, one of the most picturesque figures in history, became Czar in 1689, the very year of the Glorious Revolution in England. Europe was extending its tentacles over the world. The great continent of Africa was being opened up; the Huguenots had established themselves at the Cape; the Dutch built colonies at Natal and on the Gold Coast. Our American possessions were seeking the renewal of Royal charters; the East India Company was formed in 1691. Soon, in the reign of Queen Anne, Marlborough would be winning his great victories in the Netherlands.

Epoch-making movements on the part of nations, armies and governments were reflected in the social and cultural life of the people. It was the period of Fénélon and Bossuet in France, and of Dryden, Swift and Defoe in this country. Isaac Newton published his *Principia* in 1697; plate glass was invented by Abraham Thevant in the following year; Newcomen built the first steam engine in 1704; Lloyds' coffee house became a centre for marine insurance in 1692; the National Debt was started in '93 and the Bank of England was founded in '94. It was the period of Purcell's music; William Penn was writing on universal peace and proposing his scheme for European federation; Locke published his *Treatise on Civil Government* in '89. In the sphere of religion it was the time of the origin of many societies, some of which have continued to the present day. Thomas Bray was instrumental in the founding of the S.P.C.K. in '99, and was the main instigator in the creation of its daughter society, the S.P.G., in 1701. This list should remind us of the general character of the period, and shows that, so far from being a static age, the eighteenth century was an epoch of great activity in every sphere of human life.

III

The root of the trouble, so far as the Nonjurors were concerned, was bedded deep in a threefold principle—divine right, non-resistance and passive obedience. The first sprang from the belief that the monarchy was purely hereditary. The accident of birth alone gave the individual the right to be king. It followed that all power resided in the monarch.

He was above the law and the constitution, both of which really sprang from him. Pope's witticism about "the Right Divine of Kings to govern wrong" may seem absurd to us, but in fact was the over-ruling principle. The monarchy was of divine ordinance. The king reached his office by hereditary descent, and his right to rule carried with it freedom to insist upon the complete execution of his own will. This inevitably involved for all his subjects the bounden duty, if not of active obedience, at least of non-resistance. If his people did not like what the king insisted upon they must not openly rebel. No one had the right to take up arms against the Lord's anointed. If, therefore, the king insisted upon something which was obviously bad and inexpedient, even if it was contrary to the will of God, there must be no active resistance. All that an unwilling people could do was to submit. If they could not actively obey, at any rate they could offer a passive obedience. Unlawful commands need not be actively furthered, but they must not be actively resisted.

All this, it was held, had been actually pledged by the subjects in their oath of allegiance. It is what is known as the Stuart theory of divine right and it was held to be embodied in the oath, which was not merely official but personal. In the period with which we are dealing, all those who had taken the oath had pledged their recognition of James II as rightful and lawful king. His authority was in his person and not in the law. This can be seen from the form of the oath as it had been administered to recusants in the reign of the first James. " I A.B. do truly and sincerely acknowledge, profess, testify and declare in my conscience before God and the world, that our sovereign lord King James is lawful and rightful king of this realm and all other His Majesty's dominions and countries. . . . Also I do swear from my heart that . . . I will bear faithfull and true allegiance to His Majesty, his heirs and successors, and will defend them to the uttermost of my power against all conspiracies and attempts whatsoever, which shall be made against his or their persons, their crown and dignity." The exceedingly drastic form of this oath will be noticed. Phrases familiar to us to-day, which would, to some extent, tone down the sharp severity of its terms are conspicuous by their absence. There is no such phrase as " in all things lawful and honest " or " according to law," much less is there any mention of " true and canonical obedience."

It may be asked why such an oath should be demanded, and why the source of all authority should thus be found in the person of the monarch. The answer is that at this stage in constitutional history only two other sources of authority could be considered, and both had already been rejected by Englishmen. The first of the two alternatives was the Pope. But the Church of England actually owed its separate existence to the rejection of the Papacy, and that rejection had been just as much an act of the realm as of the Church. Only a few Roman Catholics would have considered that alternative at all, and they of course were under suspicion none the less grave because the reigning monarch himself was of their faith.

The second possibility would have been to say that the source of authority lies in the people. But again the Church of England had rejected that source, when it was represented by the Commonwealth. Never since the Restoration had any considerable proportion of the people wished to go back to that theory of government. Even if a number of secular leaders were trying to find some way in which the law or will of the people could be made to take precedence over the person of the king, it was hardly likely that the Church of England, which had been the chief sufferer under the Commonwealth, would support their point of view. Indeed, it was possible for religious men to point back to the Elizabethan homily of 1569 which laid down this doctrine of divine right, non-resistance and passive obedience as being incumbent upon everybody in the State. That homily had definitely derided the suggestion that subjects should judge their prince. " What a perilous thing was it to commit unto the subjects the judgment, which prince is wise and godly and his government good, and which is otherwise; as though the foot must judge of the head; an enterprise very heinous and must needs breed rebellion." In the period with which we are dealing there were those like Bishop Lake of Chichester who said that this doctrine of passive obedience was the distinguishing feature of the Church of England. Others like Ken and Kettlewell, when things went wrong and passive obedience brought them great suffering, did not shrink from calling it the doctrine of the Cross.

However, it should be realized that this doctrine did not mean complete subservience to the will of the monarch. The greatest moment of ' passive obedience ' had occurred when James II ordered the bishops to publish his Declaration of Indulgence throughout their dioceses. This indulgence with its specious air of universal toleration had been detected as a means of bringing back Roman Catholicism. Seven bishops, with Sancroft, the Archbishop of Canterbury, at their head, had refused to publish it. For that they had been sent to the Tower. When, however, they were brought to trial they had been released. The excitement on that occasion was tremendous. Bonfires were lighted, a medal was struck, and the nation was united behind the leadership of its Church as it had never been before. This was the real beginning of the Glorious Revolution. Secular leaders used the enthusiasm to overthrow the regime. The bulk of the clergy, in fear of Romanism, joined in the declared and open opposition to James. William was invited over. For the mass of the nation the logic of events had proved too strong for the theory.

IV

William landed at Torbay on November 5th, 1688. He immediately published a declaration giving his reasons for coming into the country. He wished to preserve the religion and liberties of the people, and he had been invited to do so by several of the Lords spiritual and temporal. On hearing of this, King James sent for Sancroft and the bishops to ask them what part they had had in inviting William to this country. They all denied that they had had anything to do with it whatever, but I am afraid that in the case of one of them, Compton, Bishop of London, the denial was inaccurate. He and he only among the bishops had signed the invitation to William. Sancroft and the other bishops knew nothing of this. However, when the King asked them to sign a paper declaring their abhorrence of the invasion, they refused to do that also.

William's path was made all the easier when on December 11th James fled from London, dropping the great seal into the Thames on the way. Later, on the 22nd, he left the kingdom altogether. Everything possible was done by William and the Government to give an air of legality to the next steps in the revolution. James had already dissolved Parliament in July. There was therefore no authoritative assembly to deal with the situation. William summoned the peers and such members of Charles II's old Parliament as were in London, together with the London aldermen. This quite irregular assembly advised William to summon a 'Convention' of the estates of the realm. The Lords were invited to join in together with representatives of the counties and boroughs. Upon this 'Convention' rested the duty of deciding what should be done. The Commons had no difficulty in resolving that James had abdicated and that the Throne was therefore vacant. The Lords, however, were not nearly so clear. They hesitated whether to declare a vacancy in the Throne or to invite William merely to act as Regent. Finally, however, they decided in the same sense as the Commons. They knew that William would not be content with anything less than the Crown. His great ambition was to defeat the designs of Louis XIV on the Continent, and he felt that he would have his best chance of achieving that end as King of England. But the vote was only carried in the Lords by a majority of three. The Archbishop of York with eight other bishops voted for a Regency; and only two, London and Bristol, voted with the majority. Sancroft and several of the other bishops were not present. If they had been, they would have turned the scale, and the history of our country might have been very different.

On February 13th both Houses waited on William and Mary, and offered them the Crown accompanied by the Declaration of Rights. The Crown having been accepted, the 'Convention' passed an Act declaring itself to be the Parliament of England. A new Parliament was not summoned until March of the following year, and that of course was done in accordance with the proper form by writs from the King and Queen. It passed a statute declaring that William and Mary were King and Queen of England, and that the statutes made by the 'Convention' were and are laws and statutes of the Realm.

In spite of the somewhat complicated steps to preserve the appearance of legality, it is quite obvious, and every lawyer would agree, that the thing was not and could not be done in accordance with the law. It was a revolution and it is difficult to see how a revolution could be undertaken constitutionally. The logical step would have been for everybody to recognize the fact and to admit that what was done had to be done and that necessity knows no law. A number of the bishops, however, could not accept that view. They felt bound by their oath to James. That oath they believed had been given under divine sanction and nothing could excuse them from the consequences of it. They had been quite willing to accept William as Regent. They could not, without breaking their oath, accept him as King. Therein lay the whole subsequent tragedy.

To us, from our point of vantage, the position seems clear enough, but it was not nearly so clear to the actors in the drama. The confusion was made worse confounded by the state of parties. One would have thought that the Dissenters would have been entirely on the side of William, but in point of fact they had supported James. No doubt they had allowed themselves to be deceived by James's specious offer of indulgence. William Penn had committed himself to the view that nothing could over-ride James's legal right. In fact if the Dissenters had had their way the country might have been handed over to Popery. William had to recognize that, whatever might be the attitude of bishops, it was the Church of England that had made his accession to power possible. The attitude of the Roman Catholics was as unexpected as that of the Dissenters. Pope and Emperor alike were prepared to assist Protestant William in his opposition to Catholic Louis of France. A good deal of financial backing had come through the hands of the Emperor to support the expedition, and it is calculated that William had at least 4,000 Papists in his army, as many as James himself could command.

In such circumstances it is hardly surprising that the Revolution put an end to the imposing unity of the Church of England. A number of the bishops found it impossible to transfer their allegiance. The difficulty was recognized, and an effort was made to meet it by giving a new form to the oath. This was proffered in the words, " I A.B. do sincerely promise and swear to bear true allegiance to Their Majesties, King William and Queen Mary." The swearer was not asked to say that they were the " lawful and rightful " monarchs, nor was any mention made of their successors. In other words people were expected to accept William as King *de facto,* but not necessarily *de jure.* They were permitted to acknowledge the fact of his Kingship without expressing any opinion as to his right. A more innocuous oath could not be conceived. It was felt of course that the position of the Crown would have been altogether too insecure if there were not some oath of allegiance. It may still be doubted, however, whether the Government was wise in expecting everybody to take it. It was known of course that there would be opposition, and it would probably have been an act of true statesmanship to impose the oath only on new appointees to office. In that case all the bishops would probably have continued to fulfil their functions.

As it was, five of the prelates from among the famous seven who had gone to the Tower for their resistance to James, found it impossible to take even this lighter form of oath to his successor. They were Archbishop Sancroft, Bishop Ken of Bath and Wells, Turner of Ely, Lake of Chichester and White of Peterborough. They were joined in their refusal by four others, Cartwright of Chester, Frampton of Gloucester, Lloyd of Norwich and Thomas of Worcester. They were followed by 400 of the clergy of England and by practically the whole of the Scottish bishops and clergy, together with one Irish bishop, Sheridan of Kilmore. Matters were not rushed. They were given plenty of time to think things over. Only when they proved recalcitrant, they were informed that they would be suspended if they had not taken the oath by August 1st. If they did not prove amenable within six months from that date, they would then be deprived.

In the meantime arrangements had to be made for the Coronation. That was actually performed by Compton of London who acted under a commission from Archbishop Sancroft.

V

The bishops in Scotland had done what they could to put themselves right with William. As soon as the news of his arrival reached them, they sent Rose, the Bishop of Edinburgh, to London to secure William's help against the 'rabbling' of the clergy, who had been suffering a good deal at the hands of the Scottish Presbyterians. He was assured that William was now fully aware that the majority of the nobility and gentry in Scotland were for Episcopacy. He was further assured that William also would support Episcopacy if the bishops would help him. At an interview William said to Rose, "I hope you will be kind to me." Rose must have prepared his answer. Although taken aback he said at once, "Sir, I will serve you so far as law, reason or conscience shall allow me." This was a fair indication to William that he could not look for much active assistance from the Scottish bishops.

After the Convention had settled the question of the Crown, many of the Scottish clergy refused to pray for William and Mary, and were consequently evicted. Episcopacy was formally disestablished in Scotland in July, 1689. Nine months later, April, 1690, sixty Presbyterian ministers, who had been evicted on Charles's restoration in 1661, were restored to their livings. In May the Westminster Confession was approved as the doctrine of the Scottish Church, and in June the Presbyterian form of government was ratified by William, Mary and the three estates.

VI

In the meantime the situation was still doubtful in England. The bishops and clergy who refused to take the oath, ' non-swearers ' or ' Nonjurors,' as they were called, were duly suspended and ultimately deprived. The vacant sees, how-ever, were not filled at once. It was still hoped that some way might be found out of the *impasse*. The chief difficulties were two. First with regard to the oath. As we have seen, the oath of allegiance was not normally imposed on persons already in office. Efforts were made to induce the Government to forego the oath in the case of men who, while not prepared actively to support the new regime, were nevertheless recognized as extremely unlikely to do anything to oppose it. It was even suggested that some form of bail might be accepted. In the Diocese of Norwich the clergy offered to become sureties for the good conduct of their Bishop Lloyd. It was also suggested that an Act of Parliament should be passed giving special relief from the oath in the case of such persons. Obviously the Church was just as much concerned over the issue as the government. If all the bishops had felt the same difficulties as the Nonjurors, it would have meant that Episcopacy would have been lost to the national Church. Those who did take the oath were acting not necessarily out of motives of self-interest, but out of a real desire to do their best both for the Church and for the country. All the sincerity was not on one side.

The second difficulty was with regard to the State Prayers, the ' Immoral Prayers ' as the Nonjurors called them. One of the first acts of the Government after the Convention had been to insert the names of William and Mary into the State Prayers in place of those of James and the Royal Family. It was obviously difficult for those who could not take the oath to repeat the Prayers in their new form. The question was then raised whether the bishops and clergy who did not like them could be allowed to leave them unsaid. The laity who sympathized with the Nonjurors' position were not in so difficult a case. They did not have to read the Prayers but only to be in church when they were read. They adopted various ways of salving their conscience. Some just refused to say Amen at the end of the Prayers. Some took into church books printed before the Revolution containing the old Prayers and the old names. Some showed their dislike of the Prayers by refusing to kneel while they were being read. Still others took snuff at the appropriate moment. That was a resource which was not open to the bishops and clergy. They could not sneeze the prayers away.

There is of course no doubt that the bishops and clergy in refusing to take the oaths were acting in strict accord with their conscience. They were devout and holy men, indeed the very cream of the ministry at that time. It is possible that their humility disguised from them the fact that in satisfying their own conscience they might still be doing harm to the Church. No one could accuse them of insincerity, because they were showing themselves ready to give up all their worldly prospects and in some cases all their worldly means. Nevertheless by isolating the men of strongest Church principles and allowing them to withdraw from the Church of the country, they were laying the whole field open for William's scheme of latitudinarian comprehension. William had long played with the idea of a wide scheme of Church union which would disregard niceties of doctrine and details of organization, and would bind all non-Roman Christians together in a loose confederation. The fact that the Revolution ushered in a period of Whig dominance in the State and a succession of Whig bishops, with latitudinarian sympathies, in the Church, shows how very serious this danger was. (*Value Judgement!*)

We have already pointed out that if the Nonjuring bishops had carried the rest of their colleagues with them, then the

Episcopal succession would have inevitably been lost to the national Church. In point of fact, however, the Nonjuring bishops showed little tendency to proselytize even among their own brethren. They accepted the fact that some were conscientiously able to take the oath, while they themselves could not. In the doctrine of non-resistance and passive obedience they found justification for preserving their *non-possumus* attitude. They would accept deprivation, if it came, with the mildest of protests, and then they would retire into insignificance.

[margin note: Yes but they called the 'Jurors' heretics.]

What they actually did succeed in doing was to cause a schism. This of course was not their intention, nor did the government wish to press matters so far. There were, however, forces at work which prevented any kind of reconciliation. The Dissenters were now as ready to support William as earlier they had been to support James. Forgetting entirely the action of the seven bishops, they now roundly accused the non-swearing clergy of Popery. There were also influences within the Church itself, which encouraged the adoption of extreme measures. Burnet, the Bishop of Salisbury, was anxious to have the oath enforced, and was impatient of delays. He in fact was too extreme for Parliament. In a pastoral letter to his clergy he went so far as to base William's title upon the right of conquest. " The success of conquest," he said, " gives a lawful title to that which is acquired in the progress of it." This was a view taken in an anonymous pamphlet entitled " King William and Queen Mary—Conquerors." When the pamphlet was brought before Parliament in 1692, Burnet's pastoral letter was considered at the same time. The Lords cried " Burn it." Whether the condemnation was due to their Lordship's enjoyment of their own pun or to their determination not to accept the view that William had conquered his kingdom, was doubted at the time. The constitutional issue, however, was so important that we may regard the condemnation as both deliberate and correct.

A further untoward incident either induced the government or allowed it to take the more extreme view. Shortly before the expiration of the period of grace allowed for the Nonjuring bishops to make up their mind, an alleged plot against the government was discovered. A certain Mr. Ashton was found in possession of a number of documents including treasonable correspondence with James. They had apparently belonged to Lord Preston and been dropped by him. Whether Ashton knew of the plot or not it is difficult to say, but at least he refused to betray Lord Preston. In the end both were convicted. Two of the letters were alleged to have been written by Turner, the Bishop of Ely. Turner, realizing the seriousness of the situation, absconded. A proclamation was issued for his arrest sometime after, but it was never put into execution. The fact that he was allowed to remain in peace suggests that the Government was not at all sure of its case. Preston and Ashton, however, were executed. They were attended on the scaffold by two Nonjuring clergymen, of whom one named Collier was himself twice imprisoned and once outlawed for his principles. Great umbrage was taken by the Government supporters at this alleged condonation of treason, and no opportunity was neglected of calling attention to it. The immediate importance of arousing so much feeling was that it gave the Government an excuse not only for depriving the Nonjuring bishops of their sees, but also for filling the vacancies when they occurred.

Three of the Nonjuring bishops, Thomas, Cartwright and Lake had already died. This left six of them to be dealt with. On February 1st, 1690, Sancroft, Turner, Frampton, White and Ken were declared deprived of their sees by Act of Parliament. Lloyd of Norwich, who had been one of the most active of them, had already been refused the benefit of sureties offered by his clergy. This Act of deprivation added what was called a Church point to the State point which already formed the ground of quarrel. The State point of course was the oath of allegiance. The Church point was the alleged illegality of depriving bishops of their sees by an Act of Parliament without recourse to any ecclesiastical synod.

The question of legality is a difficult one. A distinction has to be drawn between a bishop's orders and his jurisdiction.

His orders are conferred at his Consecration. They are the business of the Church alone. No secular authority could possibly tamper with them. But a bishop's jurisdiction has often in the history of the Church been conferred upon him by agreement with secular authority. Of this system the custom in England was and is a conspicuous example. It was argued by some, though not all, of the Nonjurors that the secular authority had no more right to interfere with jurisdiction than with orders. The rest of the nation, however, felt that what secular authority had given it could take away. It was held, therefore, that their deprivation was good in both civil and ecclesiastical law. The bishops were not of course the only people affected by the deprivation. As we have already seen, about 400 of the beneficed clergy, having refused the oath, were compelled to leave their cures.

VII

For the most part the clergy thus deprived left their homes quietly and retired into obscurity. Archbishop Sancroft was an exception. He refused to leave Lambeth. The government did not interfere with him at once, hoping that he would retire quietly. The situation in the primatial household must have been curious, because the Archbishop's own chaplains remained in attendance upon him, although they themselves had taken the oath to William and Mary. He still remained in his palace even after his successor had been duly nominated. The Government then proceeded by a process of ejectment. Judgment was given against him on June 23rd. On that day, rather than face a forcible eviction, the Archbishop left the Palace and retired to his native village of Fressingfield, which he never left again.

Bishop Ken of Bath and Wells, on the other hand, contented himself with making a formal protest in his cathedral and then withdrawing from the palace. The leader of the clergy, Dr. Hickes, Dean of Worcester, who had been one of the more violent in the expression of his opinions, wrote out an elaborate protest which he nailed to the door of his cathedral before he finally withdrew.

The Government were thus left with a number of sees and other offices on their hands. Would they leave them vacant or would they proceed to fill them? That was a very important question, because so long as they were left vacant it could hardly be said that a schism had been caused. It was always hoped that the bishops, seeing that their cause was hopeless, would ease the position by resigning. The bishops, however, were not at all convinced that their cause was hopeless. The position of William and Mary was by no means secure, and they felt that there was always the chance that he whom they deemed the rightful king would come into his own again. A similar restoration had happened before in the history of the House of Stuart, and it might happen again.

When the Government at last made up its mind to fill the vacant sees they found it extremely difficult to persuade clergy of eminence to accept them. Even men who had not scrupled to take the oath could still not bring themselves to occupy sees rendered vacant by secular deprivation. Of such perhaps the most important was Sharp, who was asked to go to Canterbury, and did afterwards become Archbishop of York. Beveridge, too, who was one of the most learned and able men of the time, refused to go to Bath and Wells. South, the greatest preacher of the day, similarly found himself unwilling to accept a see of which the canonically instituted diocesan was still living. At last, after much discussion and with many doubts, Tillotson was induced to go to Canterbury. Kidder with the same hesitation took Ken's place at Bath and Wells. Twelve years later in a violent storm a turret of the Palace was blown down and fell on Kidder and his wife while they were in bed, and killed them both. Many thought that it was a divine judgment on his temerity in allowing himself to be intruded into the place of the saintly Ken.

As far as the Government was concerned the main issue was at length settled. They filled up all the vacancies, and so secured a hierarchy which was supposedly devoted to the interests of the regime. Naturally in their still dubious position they could have been satisfied with little less. But the Government might well have trusted the Nonjurors a little further. They were well known to be quiet and peaceful men; and there was scarcely one of them who would have taken an active part in any effort to restore James to the Throne. It was the uncertainty of their own position that made the Government afraid, and their fear made them act in an unnecessarily harsh manner.

At the same time it is impossible to acquit the Nonjurors of all blame. The issue on which they split the Church was a purely political one. It is true that in those days people did not distinguish quite so clearly between religion and politics as we do to-day. It is also true that the particular doctrines of divine right, non-resistance and passive obedience, had been so triumphantly proclaimed as part of the special witness of the Church of England at the time of the Restoration that it was now difficult to disown them. Nevertheless the whole question was so carefully thrashed out on this occasion that they might have been led to see that circumstances alter cases. Stillingfleet in his retort to Beveridge had made the position clear by reducing the argument of one who had himself taken the oath and yet would not accept the office vacated by a deprived bishop to the point of absurdity. " If it be not lawful to succeed a deprived bishop, then he is the bishop of the diocese still : and then the law that deprives him is no law, and consequently the King in Parliament that made that law, no King nor Parliament : and how could this be reconciled with the oath of allegiance unless the doctor can swear allegiance to him that is no king, and hath no authority to govern." Sancroft and his friends would have replied that the so-called King had indeed no authority to govern. Yet they were willing to live in the country and accept its laws in every other respect. They did not see that there was no logical resting place between the two extreme opinions. They should have seen that they must have either all or nothing. Either William was King and so had power to do what he had done, or he was no King and they had no right to accept the benefits of his rule.

It is sometimes said that what the Nonjurors stood for was the spiritual autonomy of the Church; they were asserting the rights of the Church against secular authority. In that case they should not have allowed its unity to be broken for a mere matter of politics. Many of them took the view that it was not they who had acted in the matter, but the rest of the Church. They stood where they had always stood, and they could no more be regarded as having caused the schism than the shore could be held responsible for the gap caused when the sea receded from it. They were indeed the fixed shore, and in their own thinking remained the only true Church of England. Many of them actually went so far as to say that the national Church itself was in schism, although Ken and Frampton would never associate themselves with that point of view. People like Hickes went even further and denied to the 'swearing' Church the benefits of the Incarnation. Such men, however small their numbers became, still regarded themselves as the only true representatives of Catholic Christianity in this land. Sancroft and his friends could have destroyed that illusion by a single act. If the bishops had only resigned, every one would have admired their constancy and the Church would have been free, but as they persisted in considering themselves the only rightful possessors of their sees their attitude inevitably appears that of the dog in the manger. What they did not realize was that by making ecclesiastical organization look absurd they were opening the gate wide for an extreme reaction against it. That came quickly with the pronouncement by Hoadly, Bishop of Bangor, that the true Church of God had, and ought to have, no material constitution whatsoever.

If we ask what was the real reason for the Nonjuring bishops' attitude, I think we are bound to say that they misunderstood the proper nature of an oath of allegiance. To them it was a personal pledge and therefore remained in force so long as the individual to whom it was made continued to live. It was the doctrine of divine right that made the thing so absolute. The hereditary monarch was still King, behave he never so badly. That meant that you could have no relief from your oath. To-day we assume the existence of a higher authority than that of the King. Both in Church and State we recognize a qualification in a pledged obedience. It is ' canonical,' that is to say according to the canons or rules of the game. If the bride pledges obedience to the bridegroom, it does not imply that she will put her head into the fire if he orders her to do so. Her obedience is subject to the natural and spiritual law of marriage. Similarly we promise obedience to our superiors only " in all things lawful and honest." Or we promise allegiance to the King, his heirs and successors " according to law."

If the oath could have been interpreted by the Nonjurors in that spirit there would probably have been no schism. The odd thing is that nobody seems to have thought that way. All the arguments put up by the Government and by the ' swearing church ' showed not how the oath ought to be interpreted but how it might be disregarded. And that was a thing which the Nonjurors' conscience would not allow them to do.

CHAPTER II

THOMAS KEN AND HIS FRIENDS

I

HAVING traced the origins of the Nonjuring schism, we may be helped to realize the character of the movement more clearly if for a moment we abandon the historical for the biographical method. By common consent Thomas Ken was the saintliest of the Nonjurors. If we can learn to understand why such a man felt compelled to identify himself with the movement, we shall be in a better position to understand the character of the schism as a whole. We may also be given a standard by which we can judge the actions of some of the later members who departed a good deal from the position of the early leaders. To trace the life of Ken from the beginning will of course necessitate going back half a century, because he was already over 50 by the period of the schism, but that again may be an advantage if it helps us to fill in with greater detail the background of the picture we have begun to draw.

Thomas Ken belonged to a Somerset family. There is a village named Kenn, near Clevedon, in that county, with which his ancestors are supposed to have had a connection. He was born in 1637. His father was an attorney, and appears to have been at one time Clerk of the House of Lords. His mother died when he was four years old and his father followed her ten years later. Ken was introduced after that to the household of Izaak Walton, the gentle author of *The Compleat Angler,* who had married Ken's half sister Anne. One can easily imagine that the influences surrounding his early years were of the best. Judging from references in his later poems he had an indistinct but loving memory of his mother, and in the Walton family he found friends who were his constant delight. The atmosphere of the household seems to have been one of complete peace and contentment, strengthened by religion.

From these idyllic surroundings Ken moved in 1651, the very year of his father's death, to become a scholar of Winchester, which was then, as it is now, one of the best schools in the country. There he remained for five years, imbibing the very sound and humane education of the time. The tone of the school was religious but strongly Puritan. At the age of 19 he was elected to the sister foundation of New College, Oxford. There he gained a reputation for almsgiving and music, two characteristics which were to remain with him to the end of his life. He also earned a sufficient reputation as a student to warrant his appointment as tutor of his college in 1661. The subjects in which he gave instruction were logic and mathematics. He then proceeded to take Holy Orders.

II

In 1663 he became Rector of the parish of Little Eastern in Essex, but he only retained this benefice for two years, for in 1665 he was called back to Winchester to become Domestic Chaplain to the Bishop of the diocese, George Morley. The Bishop had recently been translated from Worcester, and proved a great benefactor to his diocese, actually rebuilding the lovely Wolvesey Palace, which is still in use. He had known Ken and the Walton family of old and no doubt found in him a sympathetic character. Certainly they both, the old man and the young, busied themselves with the spiritual improvement of their neighbours and with charity among the poor. Ken did not occupy himself wholly with the duties of his chaplaincy. He was too much of a pastor at heart to be satisfied with merely administrative tasks. He acted as Priest-in-Charge of the poor parish of S. John in the Soke. There he was so successful in the work of evangelization that a notable number of adults were brought to Baptism.

Some idea of the reputation gained by Ken in these pastoral

labours may be gained from a curious story of a child who appears to have been dumb and subject to fits, but who, having been baptized by Ken, within a month was able to answer questions in church during instruction in the Catechism. The story apparently emanated from the child's mother and was accepted by Ken. He actually adduced it long after in an argument with James II about the possibility of modern miracles. There seems nothing inherently improbable in the story. Granted that the child's malady was at root psychological, the incident is quite capable of scientific explanation. This of course would not exclude, but would rather emphasize, the part played in the occurrence by faith and prayer.

In 1666, the year of the great fire of London, Ken was elected Fellow of Winchester, and resigned his fellowship at New College. This did not preclude other activities. We perceive in him a curious restlessness at this time, as if he had not yet found a fully satisfying task. Within a few months he accepted from the bishop the living of Brightstone in the Isle of Wight. Delightful as was his new place of abode, he did not remain there long. In 1669 he resigned Brightstone in order to become Prebendary of Winchester and incumbent of East Woodhay in Hampshire. After three years he resigned this living also and returned to live in Winchester, resuming his work at S. John in the Soke. Perhaps it was a combination of his friendship with the bishop and his love for the boys that drew him back. The latter were always in his thoughts. He drew up for them a *Manual of Prayer* which he published in 1674. These prayers represent a strong reaction against the Puritanism prevalent in the school during the period of the Commonwealth when Ken had himself been a scholar. They give great prominence to the Eucharist, and if their tone seems a little high-pitched for the average schoolboy, they do at least relate all his normal activities to his religion.

It was probably at this time that Ken composed his famous Morning, Evening and Midnight hymns. He wrote much verse during the course of his long life, but this was the only poetry he himself published. The hymns reveal in a remarkable degree his simplicity, directness and deep spirituality.

> "Heaven is, dear Lord, where'er thou art
> O never then from me depart;
> For to my soul 'tis hell to be
> But for one moment void of thee.
>
> "Direct, control, suggest this day
> All I design, or do, or say;
> That all my powers, with all their might,
> In thy sole glory may unite."
>
> "Teach me to live, that I may dread
> The grave as little as my bed;
> Teach me to die, that so I may
> Rise glorious at the awful day."

And there is of course the famous doxology, which links earth and heaven as they were always linked in Ken's mind, and expresses that exquisite sense of gratitude to God which was perhaps his most essential characteristic.

> "Praise God, from whom all blessings flow,
> Praise him, all creatures here below,
> Praise him above, ye heavenly host,
> Praise Father, Son, and Holy Ghost."

Ken found the atmosphere of the bishop's home, in which he lived, a fit environment for these pursuits. The aged Izaak Walton was also living there with his son. The bishop had sheltered them ever since Ken's sister, Anne, had died in 1662. Ken's fellow-chaplain was his greatest friend, George Hooper, who succeeded him at Woodhay, but no doubt found plenty of opportunities for residence at Winchester. It is said that Ken was very lively company at this time, and provided the household with a good deal of music. He had an organ in his room and played music of his own composition on it as well as on the lute and spinnet. But the regime was more austere than we should gather from such recreation. The bishop was himself a great ascetic; and Ken followed his example in eating only one meal a day. He guarded against sloth by compelling himself to terminate his night's rest whenever he first woke up. If he did not sleep soundly he might find himself getting up in the middle of the night.

About this time he began to acquire some reputation as a preacher. He would from time to time be in attendance on his bishop in London. Since Winchester House was situated in Chelsea the Old Church often had the benefit of his addresses. Very few of his sermons have come down to us, probably because he was an extempore preacher. However, contemporaries of very diverse types witness to the power of his preaching. He spoke, as he wrote, simply and directly, but with a deep passion that sprang from his burning love of souls.

Ken's restlessness again overtook him in 1675. This time it did not involve a change of work but just sheer pleasure. In company with his nephew, the young Walton, then aged 24, he set off on a grand tour of Europe. Unfortunately he kept no travel-diary nor did he write long letters describing his journey. The consequence is that we know almost nothing of his experiences. Dean Plumptre in his two volume *Life of Ken* spends many eloquent pages in describing what a traveller of his type and time might have seen. Our actual knowledge of his impressions boils down to his judgment on Rome. He visited the Eternal City in a jubilee year, when by all accounts it was not at its best. In any case what Ken saw cured him of any desire, if he had ever felt it, to join the Church of Rome. There is a story that later he told James II that he had once been inclined to the King's religion, but that " the New Testament and his journey to Rome had quite cured him." Certainly in his epic poem " Edmund " he puts into the mouth of ' Mammon ' the line :—

" I only am infallible at Rome."

III

In 1679 a journey of more serious import took him abroad again. He was appointed, through the influence of Bishop Morley, her old tutor, chaplain and almoner to the King's niece, Princess Mary, wife of William of Orange. In this post he succeeded his friend, George Hooper, who had suffered a good deal at the hands of the dour and ambitious Prince. Ken was made of sterner stuff, and did not hesitate to show his resentment at the harsh and unfaithful treatment meted out by William to his English wife. He openly braved William's displeasure when he persuaded a member of the court, who had seduced one of Mary's maids of honour, to marry the lady. On being threatened with dismissal he immediately offered to resign; but William, no doubt remembering how necessary it was to keep on good terms with the English, persuaded him to remain.

The only other matter of importance that arose during this period at the Hague was an attempt to bring about some kind of union between the churches of Holland and England. William, who was not much more than a Deist, so far as he had any personal religion at all, favoured the proposal. Compton, Bishop of London, and the Whig leaders would have liked to use Ken as their agent in the negotiations. He, however, knew too much of Dutch dislike for what they thought our semi-Papalist teaching and for our devotion to the historic Church to feel that there was anything but danger in the suggestion. It was probably his opposition that caused the proposal to be dropped.

If Ken was thus prepared to oppose a foreign Prince at every turn he could show himself on occasion equally firm in face of his own King. No doubt his staunchness appealed to Charles, who made him one of his own chaplains on his return to England. The King liked to hear him preach and referred to him as " the little fellow who tells me of my faults." Charles was very fond of Winchester where Ken was still a prebendary. During his frequent visits the King was accustomed to billet himself on the bishop; and he would have liked Ken's house as a lodging for Nell Gwynn. Ken refused point blank to admit her, and she was forced to occupy a specially built apartment adjoining the deanery.

In 1683 Ken was on his travels again, this time as Chaplain to the Fleet. Tangiers had come to Charles as part of his

C

Queen's dowry. At first it was highly prized as giving command of the Mediterranean, but later it was regarded as too expensive to maintain. An expedition was sent out to dismantle it. The Earl of Dartmouth, who commanded the force, was conscientious and godfearing. Ken was recommended to him by Samuel Pepys, the noted diarist, who himself accompanied the expedition. Not even the three of them together could cope with the dissoluteness of the crews and particularly of the garrison. Ken indeed was rather too much even for Pepys, who did not like so much austerity mingled with his religion. But he was glad on occasion to seek a refuge with Ken from the boisterousness of the notorious Colonel Kirke and his companions. The business dragged on for six months and must have been one of the greatest penances Ken ever endured.

About this time Ken lost some of his dearest friends. Lady Maynard, who through her husband had presented him to his first living, and whom he almost worshipped as a saint, had already died. She had been an equally ardent supporter of the Church and of the royalist cause. She was Ken's ideal of womanhood, and he felt her loss with quite extraordinary keenness. Now, while he was still away, he lost the oldest of his benefactors, Izaak Walton, at the age of 90. Six months after his return Bishop Morley, aged 87, also died. This prelate had been quite a character. We have already mentioned his severe asceticism. He combined a Calvinistic theology with High Church views of the ministry. He was also noted for his sharp tongue. When he was nettled by the court's frequent visits to Farnham he asked whether they meant to turn his house into an inn. As a Calvinist he was strongly opposed to the Arminians. When someone asked, " What do the Arminians hold? " he replied, " All the best bishoprics and deaneries in the country." He spent his wealth on everybody but himself. We can remember him with particular gratitude in the London diocese because after the Great Fire he was one of the heaviest subscribers to the rebuilding of S. Paul's Cathedral.

Morley's death had a profound influence on Ken's fortunes. To fill the vacancy thus created in the see of Winchester Peter Mews was translated from Bath and Wells, and Ken was thereupon nominated in his place. It is generally believed that Ken's appointment was directly due to the intervention of Charles himself, who swore that he would have no one for the bishopric of Bath and Wells but "the little black fellow who would not give poor Nelly a lodging." He was consecrated on S. Paul's Day, January 25th, 1685, at Lambeth. He was enthroned at Wells a fortnight later, not in person but by proxy, for on Friday, February 6th the King died. Ken was the foremost among the bishops present during the few days between the King's seizure with apoplexy and the end. He had tried hard to get Charles into a repentant frame of mind, and had succeeded at least so far as to persuade him to dismiss the Duchess of Portsmouth and send for the Queen. He had, however, failed to induce him either to make his confession or to receive the Blessed Sacrament. Together with the rest of the bishops he was dismissed from the sick room while Charles was waited upon by the Benedictine, Huddlestone. The King then received his Viaticum at the hands of the Roman priest.

IV

James, who succeeded, was already a professed Roman Catholic. Archbishop Sancroft, who crowned him, had to omit the service of Holy Communion from the coronation ceremony. Ken, as Bishop of Bath and Wells, took his official part in this function. But he was not one who loved ceremonies. He had already caused some comment by omitting the customary feast on the occasion of his consecration. Instead of it he had given £100 to help the rebuilding of S. Paul's. Since he had actually been obliged to borrow money to pay for the expenses of entry upon his see, this seems particularly generous. He refused to display any ostentation or even to drive a coach in London. Later, when he received a sudden access of wealth on the occasion of granting a new lease for some property, he gave £4,000 to the Huguenot refugees.

This dislike of ostentation combined with open-handed generosity to the poor was soon manifested when he arrived in his diocese. The table is still used in the episcopal palace at which every Sunday he was wont to sit at dinner with twelve needy folk drawn from the neighbourhood. An opportunity for still greater charity was afforded him by the ill-fated Monmouth rebellion.

The Duke of Monmouth, illegitimate half-brother of the King, invaded England hoping that the anti-Papal interest would rally to his cause. His hopes were disappointed in July when his Somerset supporters were routed at the Battle of Sedgemoor. Ken was among the bishops who attended Monmouth at his execution on July 15th. He returned to his diocese horrified by the news of the wholesale slaughter that was being meted out to the prisoners by his old acquaintance, Colonel Kirke. Ken remonstrated with the King and did everything possible to ameliorate the lot of the sufferers. Even Macaulay, who was no friend to Nonjurors, admits that his conduct and character " seem to approach, as near as human infirmity permits, to the ideal perfection of Christian virtue."

This was Ken's real introduction to the pastoral care of his diocese. Those for whom he thus exercised his charity were opposed to him on almost every ground of politics and theology. In those days such differences went much deeper than they do to-day, but they did not lessen the bishop's devotion to his flock. His time for the next three years was much occupied not only with works of charity, but also in trying to remove the dreadful ignorance under which the majority of his people laboured. He mingled his alms with efforts to make them learn the Creed and the Lord's Prayer. He was baulked in his attempt to institute a workhouse for the paupers, but he was more successful in founding schools. He even managed to write devotional books for the better instructed. To this period belong his *Practice of Divine Love,* his *Directions for Prayer,* and a special volume of prayers for those invalids who were taking the waters at Bath.

For such labours Wells was the perfect setting. The combination of natural beauty with architectural antiquity formed a fitting framework for the portrait of Ken. The quiet pools reflecting like a mirror the massive splendour of the cathedral buildings; the graceful moat surrounding the fourteenth century battlemented wall; the house itself, the best specimen still remaining of early thirteenth century domestic architecture, with the noble chapel at one wing and the fifteenth century domestic buildings at the other; all those seem to fit Ken like a glove. There is a raised walk in the garden surmounting a grassy bank where on one side you look out through the battlements over the moat to the green fields and the distant hills, and on the other you look down across the garden to the ruins of the medieval banqueting hall. Here on 'Ken's walk,' as it is still called, the good bishop is said to have strolled in the dusk of evening composing his famous hymns. If we are compelled to believe that he actually wrote them long before he got to Wells, we can still picture him, without any violence to historic fact, repeating them to himself on many a calm evening as he paced that walk deeply meditating on the peace and glory of God.

In 1687 his peace was broken by the publication of James II's Declaration of Indulgence, and by its revision in the Second Declaration the following year. This was an ill-disguised attempt to legalize Papacy under the form of toleration for all. James had already ordered the Anglican clergy not to preach on controversial subjects. He had, through the revived Court of High Commission, even suspended Compton for refusing to silence John Sharp when he maintained that the Church of England was a true branch of the Church Catholic. Compton spent part at least of his enforced idleness in planting trees at Fulham. Ken had the temerity in a sermon at Whitehall to warn Dissenters against allying themselves with Roman interests. The advice was unavailing. The Church of England had to uphold its opposition to the royal policy alone and unsupported. Consequently it bore the full brunt of the King's displeasure.

This assertion
of P. 12. is against our
primary evidence
in y Burnet O.T
and Calamy.

The duty of distributing the Second Declaration to the clergy for reading in the churches was assigned to the bishops. In May Sancroft with six of the bishops, of whom Ken was one, signed a private remonstrance to James against his misuse of the dispensing power. The secret leaked out. Public opinion supported the bishops, and a letter was sent round to the clergy urging them not to read the Declaration. In London all the incumbents but four followed the advice and failed to read the Declaration on the appointed days. The King resolved to proceed against the seven bishops on a charge of publishing a seditious libel. They refused on legal advice to enter into recognizances and were sent to the Tower to await trial. While they were there the Queen was delivered of a son, and it was rumoured that the Archbishop had been got out of the way so that he would not be witness of an attempt to foist a changeling upon the country. The absurdity of the warming-pan story is evidence of the popular hatred of the King and sympathy for the bishops. On June 15th the latter were brought before the Court of King's Bench. When the day of their trial had been fixed for a fortnight later they were released on their own recognizances.

There is no need to repeat again the well-known history of the public enthusiasm and acclaim for the bishops. It reached its height after their acquittal by a jury who had been locked up all night without food or drink. Even the soldiers in their camp on Hounslow Heath joined in the general rejoicings. The trial had a momentous result on the future of the country. The dispensing power of the King had been broken by the passive resistance of the bishops. It was, little as the bishops intended it, the starting point of the subsequent revolution.

On the very day of the acquittal, June 30th, a letter was dispatched to William of Orange, signed by the leaders of the two political parties, inviting him to come and protect by force of arms the liberties of the people and the Protestant religion. We have already seen that the bishops as a body had nothing to do with this letter and may even have been ignorant of it. So far were the seven from any notions of disloyalty that Sancroft, in his instructions issued to the clergy in July, urged them to be loyal to both Church and King. James himself proved obtuse and obdurate. He tried to bring to book the clergy who had refused to read his declaration, but found there were too many. He crowned his idiotic behaviour by bringing over Roman Catholic troops from Ireland. When, however, he was certain of William's expected arrival he tried to win over the bishops. Ken and Sancroft assured him of their continued loyalty and urged him to institute at once much needed reforms. It was too late. After an abortive attempt to cross to England against adverse winds, William made a successful voyage and landed at Torbay on November 5th. On the following February 13th he and Mary were offered the crown conjointly.

As we have already seen, the Government in order to make the position sure imposed an oath of allegiance to William and Mary. Ken, having voted for a regency and against a declaration of a vacancy in the throne, felt himself unable to take the oath. It seems paradoxical that those who had sprung the mine that dislodged him should yet remain so faithful to James that they could not accept his successor. Nevertheless that is the position in which they found themselves. They were told that failure to take the oath would mean deprivation. After a short period of doubt Ken informed his diocese in October that he would not be able to comply with the Government's demands. There was still an interval before the axe fell. In April, 1691, he was formally deprived. After a dignified protest in his cathedral he withdrew from Wells.

on page 14

it's in Feb 1690 !!
Former Ken had date
(Suke!)

V

As with most of the Nonjurors, the immediate question for Ken was what he was to do with himself now that he had lost his means of livelihood. Many of his companions in misfortune found posts as schoolmasters, tutors or chaplains in some gentleman's household. It did not seem right that one who was still regarded by many as a diocesan bishop should be driven to earn his own living. Ken had given away in charity all the spare money he ever had. What remained to him now was £700, which had come to him from the sale of his goods—all except his books, which he retained. In exchange for his capital his friend Lord Weymouth offered him an annuity of £80 and a home with himself at Longleat on the borders of his old diocese. There Ken spent most of the remainder of his life, and there his library is still to be seen. Occasional visits to other friends, such as the Kerrys at Naish House and the younger Izaak Walton, alone broke the even tenor of life at Longleat.

It is possible that Ken would have surrendered his canonical rights if he had been succeeded at Wells by someone whom he could trust. The Government did in fact try hard to get Beveridge, one of the ablest men of the day, to accept appointment, but that great scholar shrank from allowing himself to be intruded into the see of a bishop who was under no ecclesiastical censure. Ken had the mortification of seeing Kidder, a man whom he regarded as 'a Latitudinarian traditor,' succeed him. He could not bring himself to yield his canonical powers voluntarily to such a pastor.

In spite of this Ken's attitude did not seem sufficiently rigorous to most of the Nonjurors. When Sancroft delegated his metropolitical authority, it was not to Ken but to Lloyd of Norwich that he gave his commission. In any case Ken would not have accepted it, as he felt the action ill-advised. He probably recognized that it would prolong the schism, a contingency that he was most anxious to avoid. His fears were only too well founded. A proposal was soon on foot to continue the episcopal succession in the Nonjuring line. Ken was opposed to what he called 'clandestine consecrations,' but his advice was disregarded. Hickes and Wagstaffe were consecrated in 1694, as suffragan bishops of Thetford and Ipswich respectively.

The purpose of this curious appointment was to preserve as far as possible the appearance of canonical regularity. If Lloyd was still the true Bishop of Norwich there was some

This is vitally important. — So much for the independence of the Church.

show of reason in asserting that he had the right to appoint suffragans. He even went so far as to recognize the crown's customary share in such appointments. Regarding James as the true sovereign he sent Hickes to St. Germains in order to get his permission for the consecration. James had the effrontery to keep him waiting while he consulted his ecclesiastical advisers—that is, the French Catholic hierarchy. They passed the question on to Rome. It was only when the Pope told him that he should agree that James gave the required permission.

Of the two men thus consecrated Hickes was the better known. He had always been a keen royalist. As an undergraduate he had been sent down from S. John's, Oxford, in 1659 for crossing swords with the President of the College, who was a strong Puritan.[1] This did not prevent him from returning to another college the next year and later becoming a Fellow of Lincoln. He was appointed Dean of Worcester in 1683, but refused to accept the see of Bristol the next year. He resisted James in regard to the Declaration, but would not take the oath to William and Mary. The tone of his protest at being deprived so infuriated the Government that he had to flee. After his deprivation he lived in hiding, sometimes in the disguise of an army officer, pursuing his learned studies in theology and in Anglo-Saxon. As we have seen, he was Lloyd's emissary at the court of St. Germains to negotiate the new episcopal appointments with James and was himself nominated to be suffragan bishop of Thetford. In 1699 the Lord Chancellor in reward for his services to learning issued a writ of *nolle prosequi* and so put him on the right side of the law. He lived in Great Ormond Street and ministered in an oratory near by, using the Communion Service of 1549. His theological works include *The Christian Priesthood* and the *Constitution of the Catholic Church*. The monument to his secular learning is his *Thesaurus of the Ancient Northern Tongues,* which was for long the standard work on the subject.

[1] Hickes' latest biographer thinks there is insufficient evidence for this story.

Thomas Wagstaffe was an Oxford graduate who became Chancellor of Lichfield and Rector of S. Margaret Pattens, London. He was a landed gentleman and also a student of medicine. After refusal of the oath and consequent deprivation he practised physic, " still wearing his canonical habit." He was a great friend of Archbishop Sancroft and attended him on his death-bed. Although consecrated suffragan bishop of Ipswich he does not appear to have performed episcopal functions, but continued to live as a physician until towards the end of his life, when he withdrew to his own property near Coventry. He wrote ably in defence of the Nonjurors' principles and shared Ken's efforts to relieve the poverty of the clergy.

However much Ken opposed these consecrations, moderation did not keep him out of conflict with the Government. Twice the following year he drew attention to himself, first by addressing a public rebuke to the new Archbishop Tenison for the undue adulation expressed in his funeral oration on Queen Mary, and again by going to Barking and officiating at the funeral of his great Nonjuring friend, Kettlewell. The Fenwicke Plot increased the anxieties of the Government and they desired to bring the Nonjurors into disrepute. They fancied they had found an opportunity of doing so in a fund which had been proposed by Kettlewell and Robert Nelson for the support of the needy Nonjuring clergy. Ken with some other bishops signed a letter in support of the project, entitled " The Charitable Recommendation of the Deprived Bishops." The Privy Council issued warrants against them for "suspicion of High Treason and Treasonable Practices." It seems almost incredible that such a charge could be entertained for a moment. The fact that it was serves to reveal the intensity of feeling at the time. At his examination Ken had little difficulty in pointing to charity as a fundamental law of the Gospel, and scored a strong point in recalling how he had himself exercised that privilege in the case of Monmouth's defeated troops. Nor had he much more difficulty in proving that by his appeal to

charity he was not in any wise usurping ecclesiastical jurisdiction. This decided the tone of the whole defence, and the
prisoners, among whom Wagstaffe was included, were all
released by an Order in Council, May 23rd, 1695.

VI

Ken's energies were next directed towards an attempt to
end the schism. In 1698 White, the deprived Bishop of Peterborough, died, and in 1700 Turner of Ely followed. Of the
original Nonjuring bishops only Frampton, Lloyd and Ken
were still left. Frampton's willingness to make concessions
was well known. It remained for Ken to persuade Lloyd that
the three should now formally cede their powers of jurisdiction
so that the intruders might be recognized as the canonical
holders of their sees. If this could not be done he proposed
as an alternative that they should publicly declare that at least
they were prepared to join in the ordinary services of the
National Church while still holding to their doctrine of
passive obedience. However, no one but Dodwell among the
leaders on the Nonjuring side was prepared to accept either
way out of the *impasse*. The situation was radically changed
by the death in September, 1701, of James, followed six
months later by that of William.

This might have been an opportunity to effect a reconciliation. The Government, however, in order to make Anne's
succession secure felt it necessary to rally all its forces, and
committed the folly of imposing a new oath. Most Nonjurors
would probably have accepted Anne as *de facto* sovereign if
they had been left alone, but they were now required to do
more than that. They were ordered to abjure the Pretender,
that is, to say that he had no legal right to the throne. This
they could not do. So far from being won over, their numbers
were actually increased by a small crop of Non-Abjurors.
Anne understood the position very well, and was prepared to
do all she personally could to provide a remedy. When Kidder
was killed in the great storm of 1703, and the diocese of Bath
and Wells was left without a resident bishop, she tried to per-

suade Ken to return to his former see. He, however, had now to contend with other difficulties than that of the oaths. Old age and infirmity were creeping on him and he felt unable to accede to the Queen's request. Nevertheless he did the next best thing. When the see was offered to his old friend George Hooper, and the latter had scruples about accepting it, Ken bent all his powers to the task of persuading him, and at the last succeeded. The relations between the Queen and Ken remained cordial, and in 1704, at the original instigation of Hooper, she granted him a pension of £200.

At last in 1710 there came another chance of ending the schism. On January 1st of that year Lloyd died. As Frampton had already died two years before, this left Ken the only survivor of the deprived bishops, and he had already accepted Hooper as his lawful successor. This provided an interesting situation. Dodwell had already written an important book in 1705, *The Case in View*, explaining the belief of the more moderate section of the Nonjurors that when the deprived bishops had left their sees either by death or resignation, the intruded bishops would *ipso facto* become canonically legitimate. As there would no longer be any rival claimants their possession of the sees would hold good. That contingency had now occurred. In order to make assurance doubly sure Dodwell wrote to Ken asking him whether he still insisted on his claim, and Ken replied, " I made a Cession to my present most worthy successor." This was sufficient, and thereupon Dodwell, Nelson and the bulk of the Nonjuring laity returned to the National Church.

It was the last and most fitting act of Ken's public life. Early the following year he was overtaken by paralysis and dropsy and died on March 19th, 1711.

VII

Ken's last years seem to have been spent in the quiet practice of his religion and in the writing of hymns which he accompanied on the viol to music of his own composition. His nature seems to have been almost entirely religious. With the exception of music he appears to have had few if any interests beyond his religion. That such a man could have been caught up into a political controversy and had his public life ruined by it is one of the greatest tragedies of ecclesiastical history. Controversy of any kind was utterly abhorrent to him. He could not, like so many of his contemporaries in a similar plight, find an outlet for his genius in the creation of great treatises in defence of his position. He wrote certainly, but most of what he wrote consisted of epic poems with a strong spiritual flavour which never achieved any great popularity.

The chief contribution from his pen was devotional literature. His principal hymns will probably be sung as long as the English language lasts. There is about them a simplicity which makes their intense spirituality available to all. On the other hand his prose compositions are pitched in too high a key for the average person. We have noticed that even when writing for schoolboys he seems to have expected them to be on his own level of sainthood. The same fault, if fault it be, is observable when he is writing for his less educated folk in Bath and Wells. *The Practice of Divine Love,* which is the monument both of his own piety and of his pastoral zeal for arousing similar aspirations in his flock, would probably have earned a right to stand beside Law's *Serious Call* as a supreme example of eighteenth century devotion if it had not been at once so exalted and so condensed. Even so it has some quite beautiful passages which should never be forgotten.

The book is an exposition of the Church catechism from the point of view of the single characteristic of charity. Every section—commandments, creed, prayer, sacraments—is explained as exhibiting the divine love. On that explanation are based prayers intended to draw out the responsive love of the learner. I quote from the edition of 1718, an original copy of which was presented to me by my friend, Gillie Potter, when I myself became Bishop of Bath and Wells.

"When the love of God is produced in my heart, and is set on work, my last concern is to preserve and ensure and quicken it; It is preserved by Prayer, the pattern of which is the Lord's Prayer; It is ensured to us by the Sacraments, which are the Pledges of love; and more particularly it is quickened by the Holy Eucharist, which is the feast of Love; So that the plain order of the Catechism teaches me the rise, the progress, and the perfection of Divine Love, which God of his great mercy give me grace to follow."

His love for the Church of his country bursts out in a characteristic passage which makes us realize more strongly than ever how much his separation must have cost him.

" Glory be to thee, O Lord my God, who hast made me a Member of the particular Church of *England,* whose Faith, and Government, and Worship, are Holy, and Catholick, and Apostolick, and free from the Extreams of Irreverence or Superstition; and which I firmly believe to be a sound part of thy Church Universal, and which teaches me Charity to those who dissent from me; and therefore all Love, all Glory be to thee."

The earnestness and intensity of his own love for Christ comes out in a meditation on the life everlasting.

" O thou whom my Soul loveth, I would not desire heaven but because thou art there, for thou makest heaven wherever thou art.

" I would not, O Jesu, desire life everlasting, but that I may there everlastingly love thee.

" O inexhaustible love, do thou eternally breathe love into me, that my love to thee may be eternally increasing and tending towards infinity, since a love less than infinite is not worthy of thee."

Like Sir Thomas Browne he loved to lose himself in a mystery and to pursue his reason to an " *O altitudo.*" Therefore he does not anxiously strive for a scientific explanation of the method of Christ's presence in the Eucharist.

" Lord, what need I labour in vain, to search out the manner of thy mysterious presence in the Sacrament, when my Love assures me thou art there? All the faithful who approach thee with prepared hearts, they will know thou art there, they feel the Virtue of Divine Love going out of thee, to heal their infirmities and to inflame their affections, for which all Love, all Glory be to thee."

His aspirations in that service find expression in one of the most beautiful Eucharistic prayers ever composed.

" O merciful Jesus, let that immortal food which in the Holy Eucharist thou vouchsafest me, instil into my weak and languishing Soul, new supplies of Grace, new Life, new Love, new Vigour, and new Resolution, that I may never more faint, or droop or tire in my duty."

The whole closes with a doxology which fits so well into its context and is at the same time so redolent of the earliest liturgical spirit that one cannot be sure whether it is original or a quotation from the scriptures.

" To God the Father, who first loved us, and made us accepted in the Beloved; to God the Son who loved us, and washed us from our Sins in his own Blood; to God the Holy Ghost, who sheds the Love of God abroad in our hearts, be all Love and all Glory for time, and for eternity.   Amen.

Ken spent much of his time writing verse. He probably did so almost all his life. When he was deprived he found great consolation in the habit. In his later years, when he was ill and suffered a good deal of pain, he could only find relief in this kind of writing. He actually grouped a number of poems under the title " Anodynes, or Alleviations of Pain." He never published any poems except the hymns, but carefully preserved his finished compositions, leaving behind at his death four manuscript volumes. He apparently attached great importance to them himself. If he was too diffident to publish them during his lifetime he seems to have expected their publication after his decease. The general public has not endorsed the estimate of their importance. Ken was not a poet. He did not possess the gift that enables the true poet to take the metal of ordinary speech and by a kind of divine alchemy transmute it into golden sound.

So pedestrian are his verses that it has been generally assumed that his epic poem " Edmund " was written while he was still a young man. Dean Plumptre, however, has proved by internal evidence that it must have been written after his deprivation. It aims at depicting the perfect polity both in Church and State under the guise of an account of the reign of the East Anglian King, S. Edmund the Martyr. Scenes and experiences of Ken's own life as well as his aspirations and thoughts on politics and religion inevitably find a place. There is a description of Wells and its springs, of the welfare organizations in the ideal state, even of the naval sentiments he evidently imbibed at Tangier.

> " He, to enlarge his Navy, made new Docks.
> New Men of War were always on the Stocks :
> To Mariners he lib'ral wages gave,
> Who for their King inhabited the wave."

But perhaps the best thing in the poem is the description of the ideal priest which is so good that it deserves to be even more famous than it is.

> " Give me the Priest these Graces shall possess ;
> Of an Ambassador the just Address,
> A Father's Tenderness, a Shepherd's Care,
> A Leader's Courage, which the Cross can bear,
> A Ruler's Arm, a Watchman's wakeful Eye,
> A Pilot's skill, the Helm in Storms to ply,
> A Fisher's Patience and a Lab'rer's Toil,
> A Guide's Dexterity to disembroil,
> A Prophet's Inspiration from Above,
> A Teacher's Knowledge, and a Saviour's Love.
> Give me the Priest, a Light upon a Hill,
> Whose Rays his whole Circumference can fill ;
> In God's own Word, and sacred Learning vers'd,
> Deep in the Study of the Heart immers'd,
> Who in such Souls can the Disease descry,
> And wisely fit Restoratives apply."

CHAPTER III

THE LATER HISTORY

THE later history of the Nonjurors is complicated and obscure. The history books have not succeeded in presenting a clear picture of it. Perhaps the easiest way of dealing with it will be to describe the events clustering round the two Jacobite rebellions of 1715 and of 1745, placing between them a group of three ecclesiastical movements in which the Nonjurors were especially involved. It is necessary, however, to remind ourselves that the Nonjurors as a body were not implicated in the rebellions. To have joined in any action of that kind would have conflicted not only with their general attitude, but particularly with their actual doctrine of passive obedience.

I

The hope that the Nonjurors as a whole would follow Dodwell and Nelson in their return to the National Church and so bring an end to the schism was to some extent strengthened by the death of Wagstaffe in 1712. His demise left Hickes the only surviving Nonjuring bishop. Here was a splendid opportunity for ending the whole unfortunate situation. Hickes, however, was not the kind of person to favour any line that suggested compromise or appeasement. He believed that not the Nonjuring body but the National Church was in schism. He was therefore determined that what he considered a true episcopal succession should be at all costs maintained. As a good scholar and a learned theologian he was sufficiently aware of the ecclesiastical proprieties to realize that he ought to have other bishops associated with himself in any consecrations. He knew that there was no English bishop who would give him such assistance. There were, however, some from across the border, now living in

England, who might be more compliant. Amazing as it may
seem in days when the Scottish Episcopate is so justly famed
for its regard for ecclesiastical order, he induced two bishops
who came from Scotland, Campbell and Gadderar, to assist
him.

Campbell was a member of two noble families, the Argylls
on his father's side and the Lothians on his mother's. He had
been brought up in Scotland and had received Holy Orders
there. The Scottish bishops in order to preserve their succession after their disestablishment had adopted the device of
consecrating bishops without sees. In 1711, the year of Ken's
death, Campbell was elevated to the episcopate. He lived
most of his time in London. Indeed although he was elected
in 1721 by the clergy to the see of Aberdeen he does not seem
to have set foot in his diocese. In England he identified himself with the Nonjurors although his family connections were
with the other side and he had himself as a young man taken
the part of Monmouth. After his change of heart he remained
a faithful and even intransigent Jacobite and Nonjuror. In
other words, he was just the kind of person to appeal to
Hickes.

Gadderar was a shadow of Campbell. He was a Scottish
clergyman who had been driven out by the Presbyterians. He
had settled in London, but by the express desire of Bishop Rose
of Edinburgh was consecrated a Scottish bishop without a see.
The ceremony was held in London in 1712 with Hickes
taking part, the only instance of an English Nonjuror helping
to consecrate a Scots bishop. Gadderar was a hard worker
and a capable administrator. He made a formal visitation
of the diocese of Aberdeen as Campbell's vicar in 1721 and
four years later Campbell resigned the see in his favour. In
the meantime he was naturally prepared to assist Campbell
and Hickes in maintaining the English Nonjuring succession.
In 1713 the three of them consecrated three Nonjuring priests
to the Episcopate, Jeremiah Collier, Samuel Hawes and
Nathaniel Spinks.

In spite of the effort to conform to ecclesiastical usage there were many flaws in the procedure. It was of course quite obvious that no Scottish bishops could claim any sort of jurisdiction in England. A further irregularity lay in the fact that the new bishops were not consecrated to any sees. The gesture of appointing them as suffragans was this time not even tried, because of course there was no diocesan bishop whose suffragans they could be. Nor was there any pretence to appoint them as diocesans. They were simply regarded as bishops of the Church at large. No doubt it was the Scottish example that set the precedent for this expedient.

The three men thus consecrated were well-fitted by character and learning to grace their office. Collier had been lecturer at Gray's Inn where the Revolution had terminated his functions. He had been imprisoned for writing in defence of James, and in 1696 was vehemently attacked because he had not only attended Parkyns and Friend on the scaffold when they were executed for their plot against William, but had publicly absolved them and in doing so had laid his hand on their head. When brought to trial he absconded rather than give bail to an 'illegal' government, and so remained a technical outlaw to the end of his days. At the time of his consecration he was busy with an *Ecclesiastical History of Great Britain,* the first volume of which had already appeared. But he was perhaps best known for his *Short View of the Immorality and Profaneness of the English Stage.* This attack on the contemporary theatre was warmly approved by Dr. Johnson who attributed to it the reform of the stage that ensued after the next ten years of controversy. Even Vanburgh and Congreve, after a struggle, admitted his contentions.

Spinks was an equally learned man, and of a saintliness which could be compared with that of Ken. He wrote mostly against the Romanists and the Latitudinarians. He had at one time been a fellow-chaplain with Hickes to the Duke of Lauderdale, and was recommended as a spiritual director to Samuel Pepys. In later days he managed the charitable fund organized by Kettlewell, Nelson, Ken and others for the benefit of the deprived clergy.

Hawes was a retiring person who had once been rector of Braybrooke and after his deprivation still managed to live on good terms with the new rector. He came to live in London and for some time ministered to a Nonjuring congregation in his own home opposite S. James's Palace. He appears to have been well-to-do, and in his will could even leave a small legacy to his old parish of which he still claimed to be the rightful rector.

These consecrations led to a renewed and bitter controversy concerning the whole question of the oaths. In the eyes of the Nonjurors it was still the imposition of the oaths which made this step advisable and even necessary. The controversy was still further embittered by the fact that when Queen Anne died and George I succeeded in 1714 a new Abjuration Oath was imposed. This exacerbated the feelings of those who would have been prepared to have accepted the oath of allegiance to the reigning monarch, but could not reconcile it with their conscience to say that the heirs of James had no title to the throne. The fears of the Government, however, received some confirmation in the following year, 1715, when the rising took place on behalf of the Pretender. It was perhaps inevitable that the supporters of the Government should be inclined to regard the Nonjurors as Jacobites, and of course it is perfectly true that Nonjuring opinion was in favour of the Stuarts. It is, however, very far from true to suppose that the Nonjurors as a whole took any part in the Rebellion. Indeed the leaders were very definitely against such participation. While they clung to their doctrine of passive obedience they would not encourage a resort to arms.

It is well known with what severity the Government celebrated its triumph over the Rebellion. No case called forth more commiseration than that of a boy of 18 named Shepherd who was actually executed for his participation on the side of the rebels. For a considerable period the Nonjurors were visited with increased hardship and it was made extremely difficult for them to publish their views or to make any use of the press. Hickes himself was an exception. He was no longer in hiding, having been spared actual persecution since the Lord Chancellor had intervened in 1699. He spent his time between the affairs of his church and efforts to get his great *Thesaurus* safely published.

One of Hickes' greatest triumphs occurred in the last few months of his life when he was privileged to receive Thomas Brett of Spring Grove into the Nonjuring Church. Brett was born in 1667 and so would be about 47 at this time. His life hitherto had been spent in the National Church. He had been ordained deacon in 1690 and priest in the year following. He was well connected, a person of some private means and an LL.D. of Cambridge. About 1711 he began to come into prominence as a preacher and was asked to preach before the Queen who ordered him to have the sermon printed. This was followed by other invitations, but when he ventured to preach on the subject of Absolution he brought down upon himself the critical comments of Archbishop Tenison. Brett meantime moved in the Jacobite direction. His difficulties about his position in the National Church came to a head on the accession of George I, when the second Abjuration Oath was imposed. He tried to satisfy his conscience by reading Dodwell's *Case in View*; but he found the argument so unsatisfactory that he determined to refuse the oath and to join the Nonjuring Church. He asked Bishop Hickes to hear his confession and to receive him into communion. This was done on July 1st, 1715, shortly before Hickes' death at the age of 74. There were a few other such instances at this time. On the whole, however, the oaths had more effect in stirring up animosities than in making converts one way or the other. The number of Nonjurors was still quite considerable and it is said that there were actually fifty Nonjuring places of worship in London, though this is probably an exaggeration.

II

Round about this time three interesting subjects cropped up, each of which deserves consideration. The first was the famous Usages question; the second was the attempt at reunion with the Eastern Orthodox; and the third was the first muttering of the storm that ultimately developed into the Bangorian Controversy.

With regard to the first, it will have been realized that the Nonjurors were High Churchmen. Indeed it is sometimes said that theirs was the only High Church schism in the whole history of the *ecclesia Anglicana.* They did not think that the English Liturgy was ' incomparable ' in the sense that it could not be improved. They lived in times when the possibility of revision was not so remote as it seems to us. After all it had been revised as lately as 1662, and they did not like that revision. They would have preferred to bring the Book back nearer to the model of 1549. Indeed although the Nonjurors as a whole faithfully used the Prayer Book of 1662 Hickes himself had used the Communion Office of 1549.

After his death a controversy began on the subject in 1716. The four points in which the majority of Nonjurors wanted an improvement of the Liturgy were (1) Prayers for the faithful departed, (2) the Mixed Chalice, (3) the Epiclesis, that is to say, the prayer for the descent of the Holy Spirit on the elements of Bread and Wine, and (4) the recitation of the Prayer of Oblation immediately after the Prayer of Consecration. These became known as the Usages; and on behalf of them many of the Nonjurors were prepared to do battle. Others, however, were strongly opposed to any alteration in the existing book. They felt that if the Nonjurors made such a departure from current standards they would be separating themselves still further from the National Church. As the aim of this section was to heal the schism as soon as possible, they naturally preferred to wait until a reunion had taken place before agitating for any revision of the Prayer Book.

However those who were in favour of change pressed on. Most liturgiologists to-day would agree that they had at any rate history and liturgical science on their side. Certainly the bulk of ecclesiological learning at that period was to be found in their own ranks, with the one notable exception of Bingham whose nine volumes of Ecclesiastical Antiquities is still a standard book. In the end the desired changes were embodied in a new Service Book issued in 1718. The question immediately arose whether it should be authorized for use or not. Even some of those who thought the suggested changes an improvement could not go so far as to think that they were necessary or advisable. At any rate they did not consider it worth while to postpone the hope of reunion on their behalf. However, the new book had very considerable backing. Its three foremost supporters were Brett, Collier and Deacon, and those three between them carried a tremendous weight of learning and force of influence. Under their leadership it was decided to authorize the book for use in 1719.

This led to a split among the Nonjurors, so that they actually became two bodies separated not only from the Established Church but from each other. The one body clung to the Book of Common Prayer and would not admit any innovations. They may be taken as the direct line of Nonjurors from the first consecrations. Perhaps the most noteworthy thing they did through one of their number, Taylor, was to consecrate a couple of bishops for America in 1722. This was a desperate effort to meet the growing need in the plantations for an episcopal ministry. But people in the American colonies did not like receiving their ministrations from so doubtful a source, and they wisely began to look round for a more reputable way of gaining bishops for their country. Ultimately, as we know, when they could not get them from the English Church, owing very largely to the stupidity of the Government, they got them from Scotland.

As was Wesley's similar measure

This year, 1722, is also noteworthy for the death of one of the great theologians of the Nonjuring movement, Charles Leslie. His writings were considered so important that even as late as 1822 a collected edition was published. It was later acclaimed as a herald of the Oxford Movement. Leslie was an Irishman, the son of a bishop who had held sees both in Scotland and Ireland. He had himself been a barrister for ten years, when at length he experienced a call to ordination. As a curate at the family home in Ireland he enjoyed enough leisure to pursue his favourite study and became an able theologian. His Irish blood made him a vehement controversialist but enabled him to remain on terms of warm friendship with those he most strongly attacked. He was outlawed in 1710 and next year became Chaplain to the Anglican members of the Jacobite court. He returned to England by grace of George I in 1721 and died the next year. He had been the champion of the Non-usagers as Brett was the champion of the Usagers. Leslie scored his strongest point in making it clear that if the usages were, as Brett contended, essential, it would be necessary to unchurch not only the National Church of England but the Roman Church and indeed every hitherto recognized part of the Church Catholic as well. If the usages are not essential were they at least sufficiently important to make another schism worth while? Leslie had no difficulty in returning a negative answer to that question also.

In 1727 George I died. No further Abjuration oaths were imposed on the accession of George II. As the dynasty now seemed to be established and the throne secure, an opportunity was given for the hottest feeling to cool down. This affected to some extent the relation of the Nonjurors to the State, but it affected even more the relations of the two parties of Nonjurors to each other. After prolonged negotiations they agreed upon a compromise which left their respective members free to use the new Service Book or not as they liked. The new agreement was symbolized by the participation of both parties in the consecration of Timothy Mawman in 1731. The next year an Instrument of Union was drawn up which formally made the two bodies one.

Some, however, of the Usagers still stood out. This was very largely due to the influence of the hot-headed Scottish bishop, Campbell. He even went so far as to consecrate new bishops in order that the Usages should not only be handed on but established as a *sine qua non* within their own small body. It seems amazing that people who were battling for correct ecclesiastical procedure should agree to a consecration by one bishop only. But so it was. In 1733 Roger Laurence and

Thomas Deacon actually allowed themselves to be consecrated by Campbell alone.

Laurence had been a dissenter. After travelling as a merchant at home and abroad he took up the study of theology and began to have doubts about his baptism. He therefore had himself ' informally ' baptized in Christ Church, Newgate Street. A tremendous discussion then arose on the validity of lay baptism in which Laurence found himself supported by Hickes and Brett against the National bishops. He thereafter became a Nonjuror and was ordained, ministering to a congregation on College Hill in the City. He naturally became a Usager, but died two years after his consecration. Of Thomas Deacon, consecrated at the same time, who became afterwards a very tragic figure, we shall have to speak later.

III

The second question that aroused considerable interest at this time, at any rate within the ranks of the Nonjurors, was the effort to bring about reunion with the Eastern Orthodox. It happened that a certain Greek named Arsenius, Metropolitan of Thebais, came to this country to make representation about a disputed election to the Patriarchate of Alexandria in 1716. By some means or other the Prelate made contact with members of the Nonjuring schism. After all he was looking for help and was presumably ready to take up with any one who would be kind to him. Incidentally, he needed a good deal of financial support while he was in this country, because he had brought his wife and family with him, and no supplies were reaching him from his own home. The Nonjurors used the opportunity to learn a good deal about Orthodoxy. They felt that in spirit it was more clearly allied to themselves than to the eighteenth century National Church. Presently they began to frame proposals for a concordat between their own body and the Orthodox.

Peter the Great was reigning in Russia at this time. He was known to be a forward-looking monarch and to have his eye particularly on the West. Had he not spent some time in Holland and England learning at first hand the technical devices of our civilization? Indeed the Western interests of Russia can be said to date from his reign. The Nonjurors therefore forwarded their proposal for a concordat through the Emperor. It took a long time to reach Constantinople and the Œcumenical Patriarch. When it did reach him it gave him some considerable trouble to find out who these people were who styled themselves 'British Catholics.' However, in 1721 they received a reply to their proposals. In the first place the Patriarch points out that they have made a mistake in their order of precedence for the churches. They have named Jerusalem first and evidently regard it as the Mother Church of Christendom. That is wrong, Jerusalem has only that status of honour which was conferred upon it by the early Councils and no primacy of honour or jurisdiction. However, the 'British Catholics' may place themselves under its jurisdiction if they like. Next the Patriarch objects to the Liturgy of Edward VI, which the 'British Catholics' hold in high regard. The mystic date, 1549, evidently means nothing to him. He knows of only one Liturgy, that of James. However he is equally ready with his British correspondents to condemn the doctrine of purgatorial fire which is only invented by the Roman Church for the sake of filthy lucre, and he is quite prepared also to agree with their desire to create an Orthodox Church in London. On the other hand he must affirm that there are seven sacraments instead of two, and he must insist on the Orthodox interpretation of the doctrine of transubstantiation.

The Nonjuring bishops replied to this missive in detail, trying to win over the Patriarch and his friends. However, in 1723 the Orthodox authorities forwarded to England an Exposition of the Orthodox Faith which had been composed in 1672. In their covering letter they showed that they were prepared to effect union first and then arrange agreement in details afterwards. "As for custom and ecclesiastical order and for the form and discipline of administering the sacraments, they will be easily settled when once a union is effected."

In 1724 William Wake got to hear of all this. He had succeeded to the See of Canterbury in 1716, and he was an expert in this kind of thing. In the following year he sent a dignified protest to the Patriarch complaining of his dealing with a schismatic church. In that year also Peter the Great died, and negotiations ceased. Nevertheless the correspondence had not been entirely in vain. When in 1868 the Lambeth Fathers took up the project of union with the East, it was from the statement of the Patriarchs sent to the Nonjurors in 1723 that they actually restarted the discussion.

IV

The third question to be raised was that of the authority of the visible Church. Benjamin Hoadly had long been known as the champion of the Government and of the Whigs against the Tories and High Churchmen. As early as 1705, when Rector of S. Peter le Poer, he had preached before the Lord Mayor a sermon against passive obedience and non-resistance, a sermon which the Lower House of Convocation had stigmatized as dishonouring the Church. Four years later the House of Commons officially and formally prayed the Queen to " bestow some dignity " upon him. This request was not granted until 1715 when George I made him Bishop of Bangor. Hoadly returned the compliment by attacking the Nonjurors. In 1717 he preached before the King a startling sermon on " The Nature of the Kingdom or Church of Christ."

The sermon was provoked by the posthumous publication of some papers by Hickes. They were of the most uncompromising description and aroused a storm of indignation by unchurching every one who did not belong to the Faithful Remnant of the Nonjurors. Hoadly wrote an equally uncompromising reply, " A Preservative against the Principles and Practices of the Nonjurors," in which he went to the opposite extreme by denying the doctrine of a visible church altogether, basing the whole of religion upon the sole ground of sincerity, and admitting of no possible intermediate position between his own and that of Hickes. This he followed up the next year with his sermon on the Kingdom of Christ.

In this sermon, curiously enough, he adopted the identification of the Kingdom of Christ with the Church which is customary among Roman Catholics, but he came to a precisely contradictory conclusion. So far from arguing that because the Church was a visible society therefore the Kingdom was visible too, he said that because the Kingdom was purely spiritual therefore the Church must be purely spiritual; Christ's authority is directed immediately to the individual soul. "Jesus," said Hoadly, "left behind no visible, human authority; no vice-gerents, no interpreters upon whom absolutely His subjects are to depend; no judges on the consciences or religion of His people." In this contention it is the word 'absolutely' which disguises the flagrant nature of the attack. No doubt the absolute governance is in the hands of God alone, but that there is at least a relative authority in human hands is stated in the plainest possible terms in scripture. Hoadly, however, did not shrink from drawing the utmost conclusions from his own premises. He would admit no tests of orthodoxy, and even denied the Church any right to look to the State for assistance in its efforts at self-government. His doctrine was one of pure Erastianism. Religious authority was vested completely in the State.

The reaction of the Lower House of Convocation was immediate. Its ablest theologians drew up a report which was passed without a single dissentient vote, inviting the Upper House to take action. What would have been the attitude of the bishops is not easy to say. Most of them were Latitudinarian and were in sympathy, if not with Hoadly, at least with the Government. The latter, however, was taking no risks. By a doubtful exercise of the Royal Supremacy, Convocation was prorogued. Henceforth, although it was formally summoned in the usual way at the same time as Parliament, no letters of business were issued. Thus it was effectively silenced for a hundred and thirty-five years. The Government also vented its wrath on those who had dared to attack its favourite bishop. No fewer than four of the royal chaplains were dismissed from their posts. The ablest of all the controversialists the Government could not reach, because he enjoyed no privilege of which he could be deprived. That was the Nonjuror William Law. But his story belongs to the next chapter.

V

In this instance we see how a question originally raised in connection with the Nonjurors had a resounding effect upon the National Church. It is the last occasion on which as a body. they appear upon the great stage of history. Henceforth they scarcely hold a place even in the wings or behind the scenes. Their internal dissensions reduced their effectiveness. Their numbers declined as the Hanoverian dynasty became more secure and less importance was attached to the oaths. The necessity or advisability of a certain element of secrecy gave them more and more the appearance of a sect or sects lurking in the hidden corners of great cities. Their bishops began to look a little ridiculous, as *episcopi vagantes* inevitably do. The maintenance of the clergy became even more difficult and some were even accused of obtaining a livelihood by dubious means. When the dramatist Colley Cibber produced an English adaptation of Molière's *Tartuffe* he gave the hypocritical leading role to a Nonjuror. Macaulay was inclined to tar most of them with the same brush. Even the great Dr. Johnson, who had more sympathy with the Jacobite cause than most of his contemporaries, could not speak well of the Nonjurors.

It would, however, be a mistake to take this picture as even approximately correct. On the contrary the evidence goes to show that the general body of Nonjurors, whether Usagers or Non-Usagers, were sincere and self-sacrificing people. They had by their faithfulness to their conscientious scruples denied themselves the usual outlets not only of ambition but of ordinary service to their fellows. Few, if any, of their clergy could support themselves merely by the performance of priestly duties and they were inevitably put to various forms of mendicancy in order to keep body and soul together. Whether in this respect they were essentially worse than a bishop like Hoadly who, it has been said, " cringed his way from one see to another," is at least doubtful. For the laity of course the position was very different. They could at least pursue a private career and the generally high standard of their attainment speaks volumes for the clergy who ministered to them.

Certainly the learning of many of the Nonjurors, both clerical and lay, is beyond dispute. Few antiquarians have enjoyed a greater reputation than Thomas Hearne. He was a student at S. Edmund Hall and assisted the Principal, Dr. Mill, to compile his Greek Testament. He gave his life to Oxford, finding the centre of its attraction in the Bodleian Library, of which he became second keeper. When, however, he could no longer escape as an office-holder taking the second Abjuration Oath he refused to deny his faith and resigned his post. He continued to live in Oxford, busied with his diaries and researches. When he died in 1735 he left behind no fewer than 145 manuscript volumes.

The last agony the Nonjurors suffered was the result of the rebellion of '45. As a body they had been no more concerned in it than in the '15. Unfortunately, however, this was not true of them all and some of the sufferers were closely related to Nonjuring leaders. Our sympathy is especially aroused by the fate that befell the family of Thomas Deacon. His name has already been mentioned, but we should know more about him. He was born in 1697 and turned out so precocious a youth that he was ordained deacon and priest by Collier in 1716 while still under the canonical age. By the time he was 21 he was already contributing to the Usages controversy and making himself an authority on early Christian liturgies. He also contrived to equip himself as a medical man. He migrated from London to Manchester, where he practised medicine and ministered to a Nonjuring congregation. He became a very popular figure in the northern town and won golden opinions not only among his own people but also among the clergy of the National Church. In spite of his affability he was an uncompromising Usager and refused to join in Brett's efforts to bring about union with their ' old friends.' So far from this he actually, as we have seen, allowed himself to be consecrated as bishop by the Scot, Archibald Campbell in 1733 in order to maintain a Usager succession.

The disheartening character of the task to which the later Nonjuring clergy committed themselves can be judged from the size of Deacon's congregation, which is variously estimated at twenty to a hundred. Nevertheless he gave himself to them not only in pastoral care but in studies on their behalf. Not long after his consecration he published in 1734 his *Compleat Collection of Devotions*. This appears to have become the service book of the Usagers and to have super-seded the office of 1718. It cannot have been used by any large circle. The Non-Usagers of course would not be interested in it. In any case they were drawing near the end. A new bishop named Gordon was consecrated for them in 1741 but he was the last of that line. Among Deacon's own body of Usagers there were still a few clergy ministering to sparse congregations in London under the leadership of Bishop Campbell. When the latter died Deacon regarded himself as the responsible head of the whole ' Orthodox British Church,' which was the name by which the sect had now begun to describe itself. How few they were can be gathered from the fact that in 1750 we find Deacon writing to London asking his clergy to send him precise particulars of every single one of their adherents.

To return to the '45 and its tragic effects on Deacon's family circle. The Pretender was proclaimed James III in Manchester on November 29th. The Manchester Regiment was mustered next morning, S. Andrew's Day, after divine service, in the churchyard. Three of Deacon's sons, Thomas, Robert and Charles, were officers in it, but without their father's consent. He himself seems to have adopted the usual Nonjuring attitude and to have taken no part in the rebellion. By December 7th the cause had been lost and the Highlanders were back in the town on their retreat from Derby. The Manchester Regiment got as far as Carlisle and then with others surrendered to the Duke of Cumberland on December 30th. Deacon's sons were among the prisoners who were marched south. The middle one, Robert, was ill and died when they reached Kendal. The eldest, Thomas, aged 22, survived to perish on the scaffold in London. His head was sent to Manchester to be exhibited on the Exchange. Charles, aged 17, was kept in prison many months. In the following January, in spite of the efforts of John Byrom and other friends, he was transported for life. The whole incident drew public attention to Deacon's presence in Manchester as a Nonjuring bishop. What must seem almost incredible to us is that the immediate occasion for the outburst was that Deacon in passing by the Exchange had had the temerity to raise his hat as a token of respect to the remains of his eldest son.

Deacon himself took small part in this controversy. He busied himself with the writing of his last book, *A Comprehensive View of Christianity,* which was an account, first historical and then doctrinal, of what he believed Christianity to be, based on the first four centuries and built up in the form of a catechism.

His following in London was gradually dying out and it is probable that most who remained after Campbell's death joined the regular Nonjuring line under Bishop Gordon. Deacon tried to make provision for the dwindling remnant by consecrating Kenrick Price as bishop in 1752. He was himself sinking into penury and had to be relieved by the charity of his friends, among whom William Law sent him ten guineas. Apparently he was also failing in mind and was no longer able to manage his own affairs. He died on February 16th, 1753.

Deacon's greatest contribution to the life of the Church was his enrichment of its worship. While still a very young man he had ably defended the Nonjuring Prayer Book of 1718. This does not mean that he thought it perfect. He was still carrying on his liturgical studies. His *Compleat Collection of Devotions* appeared in two parts, the first comprising the public offices, and the second devotions for private use. For this he ransacked all the known authorities, both ancient and modern. From the former he took the Apostolic Constitutions as his standard. From the latter it is probable that he used especially the book issued in 1658 to assist Anglicans who during the Commonwealth were denied the use of the Book of Common Prayer. This volume was described on the title page as " A Collection of offices or Forms of Prayer in Cases Ordinary and Extraordinary, taken out of the Scriptures and the ancient Liturgies of several Churches, especially the Greek." It has a lengthy preface by Jeremy Taylor defending the Scriptural character of the Book of Common Prayer, but offering this choice of devotions for use while the Prayer Book is banned. The devotions are, in point of fact, a good deal more ' Catholic ' than the Prayer Book itself, and the Communion office in particular follows Greek models. One cannot help feeling some amusement at the way in which Church of England leaders during the Commonwealth used the opportunity offered them by the prohibition of the Prayer Book to practise a liturgical development still closer to the use of historic Christendom. Deacon, belonging to that branch of the Nonjuring body which had discarded the Prayer Book, realized the fresh opportunity for liturgical development and used it in much the same way. This had its effect on the Scottish liturgy, which in turn affected the American. In fact it would be true to say that most of the revised prayer books in use in various parts of the Anglican Communion to-day have been greatly influenced by the work of Deacon and his fellow Nonjurors.

VI

To the discerning the '45 must have sounded the death-knell of the Nonjurors no less than of the Jacobites. There was now no likelihood of future changes to restore the fortunes of either. If it was true that the staunch Romanism of the

Old Pretender made it unlikely that either Scots or English would rise again in his favour, the rumoured Protestantism of the Young Pretender Charles Edward, who had led the '45, was too doubtful to be believed and in any case too late. It was said that he appeared in London and formally renounced the Roman Catholic faith in 1753. A picturesque story was told that while watching a religious procession in Rome he had been heard to say, " Oh that our family should deprive themselves of three kingdoms for such nonsense." But the public were for the most part ready to believe that all this was policy, and that in reality he had no religion at all.

As for the Nonjurors, as distinct from the Jacobites, their numbers were still dwindling rapidly, and they hardly counted in national affairs except as a useful bogey when the Government wished to raise an alarm. Moreover, they were still divided. Of the original line there were four bishops still living—Rawlinson, Smith, Mawman and Gordon, but the first three died within a dozen years or so of the '45, although Gordon lasted until 1779. Of the strict Usager party Deacon was the episcopal representative and he died in '53. But before his death, as we have seen, he preserved the irregular succession by consecrating Kenrick Price. He defended himself for performing this consecration alone without any episcopal assistants on the ground that in times of persecution the canonical requirement of three bishops as a minimum for a consecration could be suspended. A strange figure, P. J. Browne, said to be in reality Lord John Johnstone, son of the Marquis of Annandale, was also a bishop in this line about this time. Price maintained this irregular succession by consecrating William Cartwright in 1780. Cartwright practised as a surgeon in Shrewsbury. He finally repented of his separation and conformed to the National Church just before his death in 1799. Four years earlier he had consecrated Thomas Garnet who in his turn consecrated Charles Booth. The date of Garnet's death is not known. Booth carried on business as a watch-maker in Long Millgate, Manchester, till he moved to Ireland where he died in 1805.

Thus by the end of the eighteenth century we can assume that the schism had practically died out. Unfortunately we cannot assume that during its last half century the bitterness engendered by the schism had abated. Just after the '45 the Nonjurors published a volume of letters in which rancour against the National Church reached its strongest expression. It was pointed out with extreme bluntness that no schismatic can hope to enter heaven and it was asserted that the clergy of the establishment were guilty not only of schism but also of heresy and of 'immoral' worship. These of course were old charges and they may have been repeated now with increased vehemence in order to sustain the courage of those who felt they were on a sinking ship. Certainly the rank and file were beginning to find their way back to the parish churches. True, some of them took their old service books with them so that they need not be compelled to join in the 'immoral' prayers. But if it was a choice between the parish church and no church at all they very sensibly chose the former alternative.

At the same time it is comforting to notice that among these last remnants of a dying faith there were still great figures. Perhaps indeed the greatest of all can be seen in William Law, for whom we have reserved our last chapter. But with him we may associate one who was, while remaining a close friend of Law, rather a Jacobite than a Nonjuror. John Byrom was indeed rebuked by Law for being too outspoken about his political sympathies, but such rashness was perhaps natural in one who was a Manchester man and a close associate of the Deacons. In any case Byrom did not let his views prevent him from taking the oaths and so securing his fellowship at Trinity, Cambridge. He was an exceedingly versatile person, and he knew every one worth knowing. He studied medicine in France, but supported himself, until he inherited the family estates near Manchester, by teaching a system of shorthand which he had himself invented. Gibbon and Horace Walpole were among those who acquired this skill from him. Other friends of his were the Wesleys and Bishop Butler. His " Journals " and " Memoirs " are diaries which throw a good deal of light on the intimate life of the time. His poetry was much admired in his day, but we remember him chiefly for his hymn, " Christians awake, salute the happy morn." He also had a pretty wit, seen at its best in the quatrain in which he summed up the politics of the day and—dare we say?—his own relation to them.

> " God bless the King, God bless the Faith's Defender.
> God bless—no harm in blessing—the Pretender.
> But who Pretender is, and who is King,
> God bless us all! that's quite another thing."

CHAPTER IV

WILLIAM LAW

I

THE eighteenth century was a period of great personal reputations. Marlborough in military service, Butler in philosophy, Johnson in literature, Beau Nash in society and John Wesley in evangelism. To these we can add William Law in spiritual direction. In his own sphere he was quite the most distinguished Englishman of his day. Among the notable figures of his time he corresponds most closely to Dr. Johnson. Neither man played any great part in public activities; neither was provided with any ready-made platform. Both relied upon their writings and upon their personal intercourse with their disciples. In the case of Law this handicap was due, as we shall see, to an act of sacrificial renunciation. His genius showed itself in the fact that although he was denied the possibility of holding any public office he rose superior to his limitation. He lived in one of the greatest periods of English literature, the Augustan Age, and yet he reached an eminence that placed him on a level with Defoe, Swift, Addison and Goldsmith.

Over and above his quality as a writer there are two main points of interest in his life. The first lies in the Abjuration Oath of 1714 and its effect upon a man of genius. The second is to be found in the questioning of a singularly acute mind upon those religious issues which are always the most fundamental for the human race.

He was born just before the Glorious Revolution in 1686 at King's Cliff near Stamford, the son of a local grocer and the fourth in a family of eight sons and three daughters. At the age of nineteen he was entered as a Sizar, that is a poor scholar, at Emmanuel College, Cambridge. He tells us that

his early life had been a happy one. That it was also serious
may be gathered from the eighteen " Rules for my Future
Conduct " which he seems to have drawn up at this time.
These refer for the most part to such matters as hard work,
carefulness in food and drink, and self-examination. But some
strike a deeper note. Thus (I) " To fix it deep in my mind
that I have but one business on my hands to seek for eternal
happiness by doing the will of God." (IV) " To avoid all con-
cerns with the world, or the ways of it, but where religion
requires." (V) " To remember frequently, and impress it
upon my mind deeply, that no condition of this life is for
enjoyment but for trial." . . .

From the start it is clear that he was a thoroughly religious
person. He had in him a strong strain of puritanism, which
in at least one instance found extreme expression later, but
some element of which is essential to all true religion. From
this general attitude he never departed. Indeed we may
assert without fear of contradiction that we see in his case
as true an example of fully integrated personality as we find
in any great biography, secular or religious. He read widely,
studying the Latin classics and imbibing some knowledge of
Hebrew, French and mathematics. What is more interesting
in view of his later development is that he showed a keenness for philosophy and a peculiar fondness for the mystics.
It is especially mentioned that he had a particular regard for
the semi-mystical, deeply religious philosophy of Malebranche.
In all this he was so successful that after taking his degree
he was elected Fellow of his college. He was ordained in
1711, the year in which Ken died.

Unfortunately for Law there was a considerable amount of
Jacobite enthusiasm during the last four years of Anne's reign
(1710–14). The question of the succession was important as
the Queen was going to leave no direct heir, and it was
reported that she herself would be in sympathy with the maintenance of the Stuart line. Many people were prepared to
wait and see how the wind would blow. Law, however, felt
deeply on this as on most other subjects and could not suppress

his views. In a Tripos speech (April, 1713) he revealed his youthful ardour by asking some sarcastic and rhetorical questions. " Does the sun still shine when it is in eclipse? . . . When the children of Israel had made the golden calf the object of their worship ought they to have kept to their God *de facto* or returned to Him who was their God *de jure*? " Perhaps there is small wonder that Byrom wrote in his journal, " He is much blamed by some and favoured by others; has the character of a vain, conceited fellow." Anyway the university regarded this sermon as a definite attack on the Government and promptly suspended him.

This did not mean the end. Neither university nor Government was anxious to take extreme measures at this point, and Law himself was prepared to be as conciliatory as possible. Not long afterwards he preached a sermon in which he took the opportunity to uphold the provisions of the Peace of Utrecht, and also to say the most flattering things about Queen Anne, for whom in any case he had a considerable regard, amounting to admiration. However, when George I succeeded and the new Abjuration Oath was imposed, Law, like many others, was put in a very difficult position. No doubt the Government felt that it must take every precaution against a fifth column in case there should be an invasion. The events of the following year (1715) showed how right it was. Nevertheless, it was a thousand pities that it could not be satisfied with a plain oath of allegiance in the old form. Whether even this would have made the situation possible for Law may be doubted. Fortunately we are not left to conjecture what was passing in his mind. When the die was cast and he was awaiting his inevitable deprivation, he wrote to his elder brother George asking him to break the news to their mother, who had lately become a widow. How far this is the letter of a ' vain, conceited fellow ' must be left to the reader's judgment.

" DEAR BRO. :

If your affairs will permit you to pursue the intent of this letter you will oblige the affectionate writer. I have sent my mother such news, as I am afraid she will be too much concerned at, which is the only trouble I have for what I have done. I beg of you therefore to relieve her from such thoughts, and contribute what you can to satisfy her about my affairs. It is a business that I know you love and therefore don't doubt but you will engage in it.

My prospect indeed is melancholy enough, but had I done what was required of me to avoid it, I should have thought my condition much worse.

The benefits of my education seem partly at an end, that same education had been most miserably lost, if I had not learnt to fear something more than misfortunes. As to the Multitude of swearers, that has no influence upon me, their reasons are only to be considered, and every one knows no good ones can be given for people swearing the direct contrary to what they believe.

Would my conscience have permitted me to have done this I should stick at nothing, when my interest was concerned, for what can be more heinously wicked, than heartily to wish the success of a Person upon the account of his right, and at the same time in the most solemn manner in presence of God, and as you hope for mercy, swear, that he has no right at all.

If any hardships of our own or the Example of almost all people can persuade us to such practice, we have only the happiness to be in the broad way. I expected to have had a greater share of worldly advantages than what I'm now likely to enjoy, but am fully persuaded that if I am not happyer for this trial it will be my own fault. Had I brought myself into troubles by my own folly, they would have been very trying, but I thank God I can think of them without dejection.

Your kindness for me, may perhaps incline you to wish I had done otherwise, but as I think I have consulted my best interest by what I have done, I hope upon second thoughts you will think so too. I have hitherto enjoyed a large share of happiness, and if the time to come be not so pleasant, the memory of what is past shall make me thankful. Our lot is fallen in an age that will not be without more trials than this. God's Judgements seem now to be upon us. I pray God they may have their proper effect. I am heartily glad your education does not expose you to the same hardships, that mine does, that you may provide for your family without the expense of Conscience, or at least what you think so; for whether you are of the same opinions with me or not, I know not. I shall conclude as I began with desiring you to say as many comfortable things as you can to my Mother, and persuade her to think with satisfaction upon that condition, which upon my own account gives me no uneasiness which will much oblige your affectionate Bro.

My love and service to my sister and all friends at Moorhay.

W. LAW."

II

How Law managed to live in the years immediately following the loss of his fellowship is not at all clear. He had been a curate at Fotheringay, and he once mentions having been a curate in London. Thomas Sherlock, the Dean of Chichester, appears to have offered him preferment, but he refused to accept it, as indeed he would be obliged to do if he could not take the oath. Overton says that the only evidence of his ever officiating in church after he became a Nonjuror is a notice in the *Preacher's Assistant* that he published a sermon in 1718. It is probable that he continued regularly to attend the services of the Church, as he certainly did later, but not in the capacity of a ministrant. We know that he did not mix in politics, still less had he any part in the plots and counter-plots of the period. He was content with the passive obedience to which his conscience had driven him. His interests remained then, as always, religious and theological.

His enforced idleness gave him plenty of time for reading,

writing and thought. His genius, however, could not be hid, and presently there arose an occasion when it was abundantly displayed. We have seen in a previous chapter that in 1713 Hickes had sought to perpetuate the Nonjuring succession by consecrating fresh bishops who were not regarded as suffragans but simply as 'Bishops of the Catholic Church.' He had justified his action by asserting that the National Church was in schism and by arguing in favour of a very narrow and rigid view of church government. This had brought into the field against the whole body of Nonjurors the notorious Whig and Latitudinarian Bishop Hoadly. He asserted roundly that no constitution was necessary for the Christian Church, which was a purely spiritual society. He certainly exemplified his ideas in his own life, for he never once set foot in his diocese of Bangor.

Hoadly saw the basis and almost the only essential element of religion in sincerity. This was really to adopt the position of the Deists. If he did not deny the necessity of an Incarnation, he certainly denied the necessity of church and sacraments. "To expect the grace of God from any hands but His own is to affront Him." How then, may we ask, could Hoadly himself continue to confirm and ordain? Only by eviscerating those rites of the meaning usually associated with them. The sacraments were not the only elements of Christianity he emptied of meaning. This may be seen from his definition of prayer as a "calm and undisturbed address to God." With the effrontery of this description can be compared Law's "Prayer is the nearest approach to God, and the highest enjoyment of Him, that we are capable of in this life" (*Serious Call,* Chap. XIV). Since prayer could thus be emptied of its etymological significance it was natural that the same treatment should be dealt out to church, ministry and sacraments.

Law, from the quiet of his retreat, saw with the utmost clarity the completely subversive character of Hoadly's teaching. He came to the defence of Church principles in "Three Letters to the Bishop of Bangor." "You have left us neither priests, nor sacraments, nor Church; and what has your Lord-ship given us in the room of these advantages? Why, only sincerity." Hence Law argues in favour of the proper authorization, ordination and succession of the ministry. This indeed is a perennial issue. Is Christianity a sacramental religion or is it merely a religion of sentiment? If the latter, then of course all natural ordinances can be dispensed with. But if the former, then the natural and visible has its own importance as a vehicle and preservative of the spiritual. Therefore, when duly authorized, the physical elements of religion must be guarded with care. But the issue was even more fundamental than this. An essentially Deistic religion does not demand more than sincerity, but an Incarnation is naturally 'extended' in a church. That is a point upon which modern theologians of most kinds are generally agreed, and which is at any rate quite clearly the teaching of the New Testament. Church and Incarnation go so obviously together that even in the eighteenth century it seemed an intolerable paradox that a highly paid official of the Church should be found arguing against the very basis of the Church's existence.

It is important that we should recognize the true character of this argument because later we shall have to meet the view of Hobhouse, the well-known Quaker writer, that Law's opinions underwent a revolutionary change in later life, and that whereas in the controversy with Hoadly he showed himself a complete externalist, afterwards when he had absorbed the teaching of the mystics he acquired an inward religion of the heart. This is of course a complete travesty of the facts and could only have been invented by one who had never under-stood the true nature of a sacramental religion. At the moment it is enough for us to notice that at one bound this young writer of 31 had leaped to the front rank of con-troversial theologians. He had attacked one of the most influential ecclesiastics of the day and had exposed both the man and his argument to common reprobation. This he had done without any vulgar abuse or lack of charity, and simply by the soundness of his logic and the clarity of his style. The Bishop of Bangor had the full power of the court and government behind him, but he was defeated by a stripling for whom neither the Church nor the country had been able to ensure an office.

III

Silence descends upon Law for the next six years, and then we find him engaged in another controversy. In 1723 a certain Dr. Mandeville published his *Fable of the Bees*, the purpose of which is well revealed in the sub-title, " Private Vices, Public Benefits." It was in point of fact a re-publication with notes and explanations of a poem he had published nine years before. In it he had described a hive of bees which flourished on fraud and luxury, but lost its all when the members agreed to turn honest. It was an extreme statement of the view that the morality of actions should be judged only by their results, and was an attack on those philosophers, like Lord Shaftesbury, who taught that morality was a matter of intuition or conscience. Law recognized the poem as subversive of the whole Christian moral system, and replied to it in his *Remarks on the Fable of the Bees*. He pursued his now familiar method in controversy, ignoring details and driving straight at the main point. He refused to be sidetracked into discussions whether honesty was or was not the best policy. He proclaimed that morality was necessary to the true nature of man. Human beings were not just insects or animals. They were made in the image of God, and as God was a moral being, so they must be moral too. " If," said Law, addressing his opponent, " you would prove yourself to be no more than a brute or animal, how much of your life you need alter, I cannot tell, but at least you must forbear writing against virtue, for no mere animal ever hated it." The pamphlet, for it was little more, added to the reputation Law had already gained. He was now a figure to be reckoned with not only in the sphere of theology but also in that of moral philosophy, a field that has always drawn the attention of the greatest English thinkers. As for literary excellence the book was regarded as a model of reasoning, wit and style.

A further three years pass and we find Law engaged in a third controversy. This was probably the only one in which he did not get the better of the engagement. It is certainly the only one in which he can be justifiably accused of undue heat. It was an attack on the stage, and not on some undesirable elements merely but on the stage as a whole. The very title of his work reveals that fact from the outset, *The Absolute Unlawfulness of Stage Entertainments fully Demonstrated*. True to his title he explains his attitude without the slightest equivocation. "The stage is here condemned . . . not as things that may only be the occasion of sin, but such as are in their own nature grossly sinful."

One remembers of course the unpleasant character of Restoration drama, from which apparently the reputation of the stage had not yet recovered in spite of the improvement alleged to have followed the publication of Collier's book in 1698. Law says that within the last forty or fifty years there had not been one play "free from wild rant, immodest passions and profane language." He claims that this is the perpetual condition of the stage. There is no such thing as an innocent play. The consequence is that the playhouse is "as certainly the house of the devil as the church is the house of God." All this of course appears to us terribly narrow-minded. We have long ago discovered that the right way to deal with the stage is not to abuse it but to reform it, and the right way to reform it is to get the best people interested in it whether as writers, managers, players or spectators. We have even shown our sense of its potential value by bringing plays into the church.

How then explain Law's attitude? The fact is that it was in line with that strain of puritanism we have already detected in his character. It is closely paralleled by that of John Wesley and some other religious leaders of the period. It arose from their utter concentration upon what was specifically religious. We shall see later that this concentration even led to disparagement of all secular learning. It is possible also that Law was condemning something of which he had no personal experience. That he must have read some of the greatest plays in Latin and English goes without saying, but whether he had been an habitué of the theatre or even seen a play may be doubted. Even if he had had personal experience of the contemporary stage it would probably have strengthened his innate puritanism. It would have required much more patience than he possessed to remove the tares from the wheat. The fact is that he was dealing with one of the most difficult problems of Christian conduct, how to act when good and evil, flesh and spirit, church and world are closely intermingled. Law answered in this instance by cutting the Gordian knot and withdrawing from the whole sphere of possible temptation. In spite of the fact that Collier also had written against the stage, and had been supported by Dryden, the society of his day as well as that of ours judged him wrong. At least we can say in his justification that there are a number of gospel maxims that could be quoted on his side. What he did not realize was that his attitude was hardly in keeping either with his teaching on the Incarnation or his doctrine of the sacraments. Christianity is neither a world-renouncing nor a world-accepting religion : its aim is world-transformation.

IV

This lapse on Law's part, if lapse it were, remained unique. By way of contrast he published in the selfsame year (1726) one of his greatest works, the *Christian Perfection*. That Law himself was not conscious of any contrast is shown by the fact that he incorporated most of the former work in the new. But that is not sufficient to detract from the latter's value. It was indeed a masterpiece of the spiritual life, all the more so because it did not pitch the level of attainment too high. Perfection he explained as simply " the right performance of necessary duties." Upon this he enlarges with an amazing combination of wit, sarcasm and spiritual insight. He even introduces some of those illustrative personalities which he was to use with such effect later in the *Serious Call*. He takes religion to be, as S. Paul calls it, a serious business, indeed the most serious in which mankind can be engaged. The purpose of the world is simply to " furnish members for that blessed society which is to last for ever." There is much insistence upon the need for repentance and self-denial. Both are examples of that suffering which " is to be *sought,* to pay some of the debt due to sin." Similarly the flesh, which is the source of most of our difficulties, must be kept under by vigorous fasting. On the positive side the life of devotion is to be built upon the imitation of Christ and to find expression in prayer. Particularly " we are most of all to desire those prayers which are offered up at the altar where the Body and Blood of Christ are joined with them."

The puritanical note already mentioned is still clear in the work. It is to be seen in a surprisingly strong denunciation of all secular learning. It leads also to a pessimistic view of the physical world, whose end is merely to be burnt, and of the material body which is " a mere sepulchre of the soul." Perhaps a greater defect is the emphasis on good works rather than faith, but this may be due to the fact that the book is what it claims to be, not a doctrinal but a practical treatise. Nevertheless if we find here plenty of close parallels to those ' moral codes ' with which S. Paul besprinkles his letters, it is unfortunately true that we miss the overflowing joy that is so strongly characteristic of Philippians, Colossians and Ephesians. Perhaps its strongest point and the one which would commend it most to its own age is the skill with which the book demonstrates the *reasonableness* of the views it advocates. Thus it uses the fashionable method of argument to form the strongest attack imaginable on the low standard of religion prevalent at the time.

In any case the triumph of the book was immediate and its effect widespread. Most religious leaders used it as a quarry, and John Wesley encouraged its reading by members of his society. One mark of appreciation it received opened up a new sphere of usefulness for its author, and so had an important effect on his later life. One day as Law was standing in his publisher's shop a stranger approached him and, on learning that he was indeed the distinguished author, handed him an envelope which, when opened, was found to contain a cheque for £1,000. With this sudden access of wealth Law was enabled to become a benefactor of his native town. The next year he founded a school at King's Cliff for fourteen girls. He himself took the utmost care for the arrangement of every detail of this new foundation. Religion of course was to be the inspiration of everything taught. How closely it was to enter into the everyday life of the girls can be seen from the fourth of the rules he himself drew up for the pupils.

" Every girl at her entrance in the morning shall kneel down by her mistress and with her hands held together shall say the prayer appointed for the morning, and before they go away shall say the prayers for the evening, and at their rising up shall make a curtsey. No girl shall talk, or laugh, or make any noise in the room where her mistress is. Every girl that gives the lie to any other girl, or calls another a fool, or uses any rude or unmannerly word, shall kneel down, and in the presence of them all shall say, I am heartily sorry for the wicked words that I have spoken. I humbly beg pardon of God and of all you that are here present, hoping and promising by the help of God never to offend again in like manner. Then shall the girl that has been abused come and take her up from her knees and kiss her, and both turning to their mistress, they shall make a curtsey and return to their seats."

Of the making of curtseys there was no end. The girl must curtsey to every " matron and mistress of a family, and to all ancient people whether evil or poor," as well as at entrance to or exit from a house. In view of the small amount of physical exercise allowed to girls in those days it may be supposed that these many curtseys, besides serving the ends of politeness, afforded the same benefits as are now expected from a plentiful recourse to the gymnasium.

V

It is in this same year (1727) that we first hear of a definite change in Law's circumstances. One of the few ways left open to the Nonjuring clergymen of earning a living was to become tutor or chaplain in the home of some wealthy sympathizer. Law was now offered and accepted such a post in the house of Edmund Gibbon, grandfather of the great historian. He was a well-to-do business man who had already lost one fortune in the explosion of the South Sea Bubble and had succeeded in building up another. He had a considerable residence in Putney. There he established Law as the tutor of his son, who was just going up to Law's old college of Emmanuel. The young man was an unsatisfactory pupil and Law had small profit from his efforts, but the family did not blame him. Even the famous grandson, who was no particular friend of the clergy or of the religion they professed, could later say of Law that " he believed all that he professed and practised all that he enjoined." Indeed Law's position in the household was such that he was able to pursue his own interests and to entertain a considerable body of disciples. Many inquirers sought him out there, among them the redoubtable Wesley brothers. He was as much the ' Sage of Putney ' as a later writer and thinker was the Sage of Chelsea.

Here also Law was able to carry on his writing. In the very next year he published the most famous of all his books, the *Serious Call to a Devout and Holy Life*. This is one of the really great religious books of the ages. For human interest it is worthy to be placed beside the *Pilgrim's Progress,* but in its religious teaching it is more closely comparable to Francis de Sales' *Introduction to the Devout Life*. Law's object was that of an even more famous Frenchman, Pascal, namely to turn nominal into wholehearted Christians. He set himself quite definitely to correct the prevailing tone and temper of the time. The watchword of the age was " no excess." Against that was to be set " the uncompromising simplicity with which he adopts the Christian ideal and gives new life to common-places." He made old truths live again because he had felt

F

them so freshly and so intensely. As Gibbon said, " he exposes, with equal severity and truth, the strange contradiction between the faith and practice of the Christian world."

In his last book he had started the practice of introducing characters to illustrate and enforce his teaching. In the present book he carried the method to perfection. These embodiments of virtue and vice were not always fictitious. Some of the sweetest characters were almost certainly drawn from his own family. All alike show the keenest insight into the trials, the failures and the attempted heroisms of human nature. It is a handbook for the psychologist as well as for the earnest seeker after religious perfection.

Take for instance this pointer to what is really worth while, touched off in one brief characterization :—

" Our friend Lepidus dy'd, you know, as he was dressing himself for a feast; do you think it is now part of his trouble, that he did not live till that entertainment was over? " (*S.C.,* 39).

Or consider his famous description of a lady of fashion :—

" Flavia would be a miracle of Piety, if she was but half as careful of her soul, as she is of her body. The rising of a pimple on her face, the sting of a gnat, will make her keep to her room for two or three days, and she thinks they are very rash people, that don't take care of things in time. . . . She will sometimes read a book of piety if it is a short one, if it is much commended for stile and language, and she can tell where to *borrow* it " (*S.C.,* 97–8).

He commends voluntary poverty, virginity and devout retirement, but will not say that they are necessary to perfection :—

" Christian perfection itself is ty'd to no particular form of life; but is to be attained, tho' not with the same ease, in every state of life " (*S.C.,* 481).

Although he has no use for rationalism he is very strong on the need for reason :—

" Reason is our universal law that obliges us in all

places, and at all times; and no actions have any honour, but so far as they are instances of our obedience to reason " (*S.C.*, 498).

No wonder that Charles Bigg says of this book : " It is a splendid protest against the spiritual apathy of the times, and no more strenuous plea for consistency and thoroughness was ever delivered " (*S.C.*, XXX).

Both the Wesleys and Whitefield were strongly influenced by this book, and this it was that first made Dr. Johnson think earnestly of religion. It has been the source of inspiration, comfort and strength to multitudes since.

Three years passed in the mingled labours of tuition and spiritual direction. Law's task as unofficial adviser to many seekers after truth made it necessary, if compulsion were needed, to keep in touch with the thought of the day. The common tendency towards Deism was undermining not only the consistent practice of churchly religion but also faith in specific Christian doctrine. Everything was being reduced to the dead level of natural religion. A conspicuous example of this tendency was to be found in Tindal's *Christianity as old as the Creation*. The claim of this book was that whatever in Christianity is true is not new and whatever is new is not true. This was an unwarranted exploitation of the customary assertion that Christianity is the absolute religion. If it is absolute it is not easy to show how it can be based on a development or a break in history such as is presupposed in the doctrine of a special revelation or an Incarnation. Tindal of course rejected the idea of such a revelation and grounded religion solely on reason. The discussion was therefore another phase of the Bangorian Controversy. Law recognized its fundamental importance and came to the support of traditional Christianity with a new book, *The Case of Reason*. He did not deny that Christianity was as old as the Creation but argued that our knowledge of it was due not to reason but to revelation. The case of reason was that reason had no case at all. Man was quite incapable by his unaided intellect of discovering the truths contained in the Christian revelation. Law thus showed himself the thoroughgoing opponent of that dominant rationalism of which Locke was the great exponent. In proving the impotence of human reason he anticipated some of the most popular religious teachers of to-day, such as Rudolph Otto and Karl Barth. Whatever we may think of the points scored by either side in this controversy, there is at least this to be said, that religious conviction does not come as the result of intellectual ratiocination alone. It is a response to the leading of the Holy Spirit on the part of the whole personality. The will and the affections have their part to play as well as the reason. It is that surrender of the entire man which we know as ' faith.'

It can easily be seen that all this chimed in very well with the teaching of those mystical writers with whom Law had already made acquaintance as an undergraduate. About this time he became subject to a fresh access of this influence. He came in contact with the writings of Jacob Behmen, a German shoemaker, who had developed an obscure, semi-theosophical type of mysticism. Yet Law found it singularly attractive. " When I first began to read Behmen's book," said Law, " it put me into a perfect sweat." But he " followed the impulse to dig," and actually learnt High Dutch in order to study Behmen's teaching. The result was that his own religion took on a deeper note. There is no sign, so far as I can see, that he abandoned his former positions, but he found them strengthened and more profoundly spiritualized. As a result of this process he was himself classed among the mystics and became known as *the* English Mystic *par excellence*.

VI

There followed a period of great calm and happiness. Edmund Gibbon died in 1737. After a short residence in the Strand, where he carried on his work of spiritual guidance, Law moved to his native place of King's Cliffe at the age of 54. There he took up residence in the Hall Yard House, which had been left him by his father. Four years later he was joined by Miss Hester Gibbon, daughter of his old benefactor, and her friend, Mrs. Hutcheson. The two ladies had between them a handsome income of £3,000 a year, and the three friends set up a kind of conventual establishment, which can be most closely compared with that of Nicholas Ferrar at Little Gidding. Mrs. Hutcheson founded a school for eighteen (later twenty) boys as a companion to the girls' school already founded by Law. Together they also established almshouses in the town. To these institutions the three friends gave up a great part of their time. They also devoted to charity whatever was left over from their combined income after their household expenses were paid.

Their communal life was strenuous to a degree. They rose at five and gave the first hours of the day to devotion and study. They then distributed milk and tasted the soup for the poor. At nine they were ready for family prayers. The rest of the morning was spent in varied pursuits of management and study. At noon there was dinner followed by further devotions. The afternoon was again given to necessary duties including the visiting of the sick and the care of the poor. Tea, at which Law allowed himself the luxury of a few raisins, was followed by the reading of a chapter from the Scriptures for the benefit of the servants. Then there was a walk followed by supper and prayers. After that Law enjoyed his one pipe of the day and retired to bed at nine.

Two literary gems reflect the calm of this period, *The Spirit of Prayer* (1749) and *The Spirit of Love* (1752). These are attempts to set out in a positive way the mystical elements in his teaching. In both cases he writes a preliminary essay and then introduces questions so that each work is continued in dialogue form. The sub-title of *The Spirit of Prayer* is " the Soul Rising out of the Vanity of Time into the Riches of Eternity," which indicates that prayer is not interpreted in any narrow sense but as the whole attitude of the soul towards God. It is significant that the character who shows himself most capable of grasping the full revelation of the Spirit is Rusticus, a person so unlearned that he can neither read nor write. Christianity is depicted as " nothing less than the goodness of the Divine Life, Light, and Love living and working in the soul," and the unsatisfying nature of merely ecclesiastical questions and disputes is witheringly exposed.

In *The Spirit of Love* Law shows that by this time at least the world-transforming character of Christianity had taken possession of his mind. As matter can be sublimated into ether, so our fleshly nature can be transformed into spiritual life by the operation of the Spirit of Love in the inward man. Essential Christianity is the renewed life of Christ *within us*. He favours the teaching of Fénélon against Bossuet in emphasizing the possibility of disinterested love. The very nature of God is love and we must not be misled by passages in the Scriptures which seem to suggest that there is a wrath in God needing to be appeased. This of course affects Law's doctrine of the Atonement, which he works out as follows : (1) God is all love; wrath is not in Him but in man. (2) Therefore an Atonement is not needed to appease an angry God but to effect a change in man. (3) This is done by the communication of Christ to the soul; all virtues are thus potentially within us by reason of Christ's indwelling; they need only to be expressed in daily life.

During this period there seems to have been only one cloud. He enjoyed radiant health, as indeed he had always done. He was happy in the companionship of his friends and in the ordered life of his little community. In his works of charity he was able to find opportunity for the expression of what he believed to be essential Christianity. Though he could not minister in the parish church he regularly attended its services. The cross of his Nonjuring principles had become second nature and easy to bear. He did not enter into the controversies that were dividing his fellow Nonjurors from each other. Indeed in his *Spirit of Prayer* he seems even to poke fun at the trouble over the ' Usages ' question. The one cloud was the renewed dispute forced upon him by John Wesley. This had originally occurred on Wesley's conversion in 1738, but broke out again in 1756 when Wesley returned to the attack.

Like many other converts who have received the light of a new spiritual illumination, Wesley saw little but darkness in his past. He turned upon his old teacher and roundly accused him of being ignorant of the essential place occupied in the Christian gospel by faith. It was useless for Law to answer that it was all there in what he had originally taught. The fact was that he had not made Wesley see it and that was enough. Most spiritual directors must have suffered the same kind of experience at the hands of some penitent. There seems a strange kind of impulsion in certain types of 'conversion' that makes the subject deny even the least value in anything he has known before. The light that then bursts on him is so bright that it blinds him to everything else. However, nothing can excuse the bitterness with which Wesley attacked Law nor the absurd tone of superiority he adopted towards him. By contrast Law's own action appears that of a courteous and cultured Christian gentleman. It was not in John Wesley's nature to apologize, but time wore down his asperity and in spite of all he did manage strongly to recommend the reading of Law's books and even issued some of them to the members of his society.

The last writing that Law published was *An Humble, Earnest and Affectionate Address to the Clergy*. It was an effort to give his clerical brethren the benefit of his mystical teaching. There is nothing particularly 'clerical' in the address. Law recognized that in the last resort the clergy needed precisely the same help in their spiritual lives as the faithful laity. The one thing needful is the cherishing of the Divine life within the soul. For the clergy it is especially necessary to remember this. So much of their life is inevitably spent in caring for the machinery of Church organization; they are so much taken up with matters of Church attendance and preparation for and ministration of the sacraments that it is possible for their vitality to be dissipated in the never-ending round of routine. The remedy lies in the text, " Yet not I, but Christ that liveth in me." It is Christ, the well of life within us, who can make the whole mechanical side of existence the vehicle of vigorous and effective life. We must therefore continually return to essentials. " Show me a man whose heart has no desire or prayer in it but to love God with his whole soul and spirit, and his neighbours as himself, and there you have shown me the man who knows Christ, and is known of Him—the best and wisest man in the world."

It was not a bad note upon which to end so sincere and self-sacrificing a life. Law caught a bad cold during Easter week 1761, while busy at some work in connection with his charity schools. It turned to an inflammation of the kidneys and in a few days he was dead.

Law is judged to occupy an " isolated position in the history of English thought." His primary importance is that he stood right athwart the rationalism of his age. He was able to attack it with its own weapons and by employing all the literary and philosophic skills that were so highly admired in his day to show the insufficiency of reason and natural religion. In his emphasis on Church and sacraments he was a precursor of the Tractarians, but he differed from them in appealing less to authority than to the Light within. As he developed he emphasized the latter ever more strongly. He was clear that the external ordinances of religion were of little value without a true religion of the heart. Every churchman should recognize the importance of both. It is a pity that non-churchmen sometimes regard them as almost incompatible.

Hobhouse actually claims Law as essentially a Quaker. He holds that Law's writings fall into three mutually exclusive groups, first the early treatises against Hoadly which emphasize the Church, second the middle group emphasizing good works, and third the mystical writings emphasizing the inner work of the Spirit. He attacks his biographer Overton for maintaining Law's consistency as a thinker and writer, for not noticing that all so-called High Church tendencies disappear about 1740, that is after he had come under the influence of Behmen and gone to live at King's Cliffe, and for not realizing that Law's emphasis on the spirit of prayer and love is broad-church and Quaker rather than High Church. A sufficient answer to this is to say that if every writer were to be judged merely by the positions he maintained in his latest books we should make nonsense of all theological writing. No theologian expounds his whole position in each treatise he writes. Normally he puts pen to paper in order to deal with a specific subject or to meet a specific difficulty. Very few have the happiness of expounding the whole of their system or of compiling a whole compendium of theology. By what right then should we assume that in developing one point they have abandoned the rest? Surely we may take it for granted that if a serious writer were giving up some position he once held he would say so. In one of his latest books, *The Spirit of Love,* Law goes out of his way to remind his readers how the Established Church emphasizes the point he is himself making. Indeed it would not be difficult to show how each of the later sections of his writings presupposes the earlier. It is therefore completely gratuitous to affirm that Law, in asserting the importance of spiritual religion, had tacitly abandoned his belief in church, sacraments and the detailed rules of Christian conduct. To do so would be all the more egregious since Law continued right up to the end of his life to practise even the niceties of that churchly code that had meant so much to him at the beginning. Moreover it would be grossly to misunderstand Law's sacramental doctrine. To him the sacraments were not merely ordinances. They were grounded in the very nature of things.

That is why Law's real place in the history of English religion is with the rest of the Nonjurors as a defender of the true nature of the Church, both in its outer and in its inner life. It was they who made possible the Catholic Movement of the following century.

and have in broad-church and Quaker rather than High Church. A sufficient answer to this is to say that if every writer were to be judged...

EPILOGUE

WE are now in a position to balance the debit and credit accounts of this movement. Schism, it may be said, is always bad, and there cannot be any credit account to reckon. I hope that what has already been said will cause us to hesitate before applying so harsh a judgment. God could not allow such sacrificial sincerity to fail of all reward. That schism is a bad thing we should be ready to affirm, but there is a soul of goodness in things evil. Shakespeare's toad "ugly and venomous, wears yet a precious jewel in his head." God over-rules evil for His own purposes. It is possible to see how the Church gained as well as suffered from this unique High Church schism.

That the schism did great harm to the Church is incontestable. It weakened the parent community by drawing off a large proportion of its best men just when they were most needed. The eighteenth century church has become, justly or unjustly, a byword for apathy, time-serving, and dullness. That need never have happened had the Nonjurors remained within it. Amid the general weakness the more churchly elements in the Establishment suffered most severely. It was difficult to maintain the traditional doctrine of the ministry in the face of attacks from Deists and Latitudinarians while those who stood most strongly for that doctrine were consecrating bishops without a see and without a single assistant at the imposition of hands.

Further the national hold on religion, which was already weak enough, was bound to be weakened still further when theologians of no mean repute were busy unchurching the national church. Nor was the bulk of the nation likely to be helped by seeing how easily religious leaders could link their membership of the Church to a purely political issue. Especially would this be found unedifying when the whole political attitude of the country was undergoing a specially rapid transition. Religion could hardly benefit by being tied to an outworn political theory which was more and more obviously left behind. The total effect of the schism was thus to weaken religion in the country.

To the Church perhaps the heaviest blow was the virtual suppression of Convocation. If it is unfair to attribute this disaster directly to the Nonjurors, at least we cannot help remembering that the publication of Hickes' papers was the occasion for the dispute which resulted in the silencing of the Church's own governing body. If the Nonjuring case had not been so baldly stated, Hoadly could not have written so extreme a reply: the dispute would not have been so bitter and the Government would have had less excuse to interfere.

If all this must be said on one side of the account there is much to be said on the other. We may believe that Providence will always bring some good result out of pure conscientiousness, however mistaken it may be. Here were men who were ready to give their all in support of their honest conviction. In a world which was full of Vicars of Bray this must have told heavily in favour of true religion. These men, having thus surrendered all means of worldly advancement, could demand a respectful hearing when they spoke of the need of wholeheartedness in religion. Their sacrificial sincerity was a standing rebuke to the indifference and lethargy of the age.

Further they conferred a benefit on the State by forcing consideration to be given to the precise meaning of the Oath of Allegiance, and similar oaths. It was indeed lamentable that the lawyers of the period did not take up the question and deal with it openly and fully, although we can realize the embarrassing nature of the task. To make things worse by adding an Abjuring Oath was a blunder of the worst type. Nevertheless the inevitable reaction of sympathy towards quite good and sincere men who suffered for their inability to take these oaths, did ultimately lead to enlightenment on the true nature of such obligations. One can hardly conceive that the same kind of difficulty would be likely to arise again.

The Church, which suffered more from the schism than did the State, can still find some compensation for the wound inflicted. The Nonjurors did in effect, though not originally in theory, show the Church's independence of the State. This may seem at first sight odd when it is remembered that the Nonjurors were suffering for their loyalty to the King who was Supreme Governor of the Church. But the fact is that once the break occurred it was no longer possible for them to think of the Church as the nation on its spiritual side. Hooker's position became impossible for them. They inevitably built up a doctrine of the Church as a separate entity—as Law did in his controversy with Hoadly. This of course was in fact the original doctrine of the Church during the age of persecution. Its revival was to mean a great deal when it had been taken over by the theologians of the establishment. It was on this doctrine that the Oxford Movement was founded.

It followed naturally from their attitude of detachment that the Nonjurors took a tremendous interest in Christian antiquity. Only Bingham in the opposite camp was able to compete with them. Their interest settled very largely in questions of worship. They were far and away the greatest liturgiological scholars of their period. But what was equally important was their ability to carry out the experiments that their studies suggested. If they had still been in the Established Church under the rigid uniformity then prevailing they would have had no opportunity to try out their ideas in practice. And so, unless indeed Scotland could have supplied the lack, the improvement in forms and methods of worship which has characterized later Church history both in the British Isles and overseas would have been well-nigh impossible. It was their freedom that gave them the opportunity to experiment.

Similarly the freedom enjoyed by the Nonjurors enabled them to begin breaching the wall of isolationism that had for too long cut off the Church of England from the rest of Christendom. They naturally looked round for allies, and it was a sound instinct that led them to seize a favourable opportunity to open up negotiations with the Eastern Orthodox. Our present cordial relations with those churches owe more than is generally realized to the beginning first made by the Nonjurors.

On the more strictly doctrinal side the Nonjurors prepared the way for the later Catholic Revival by their emphasis on the sacraments. That emphasis, as we see in the case of Ken, arose out of a deep personal experience of the strength and comfort to be found in this element of Christian worship. Doctrinally they were quite clear that however strongly they believed in a Real Presence they must with equal strength repudiate the teaching of transubstantiation. Their insistence on the duty of frequenting the sacraments might have become cold and moralistic had not a superb rationale of it been supplied by the mysticism of William Law. For him the sacraments connoted the importation of the life of Christ to the believer. This ensured that the outward ordinances of religion should not be mere items in a code but the integument of a living, throbbing vitality that was communicated to the soul of the believer. And that vitality was the life of Christ—not only of the historic Christ of 2,000 years ago nor of the cosmic Christ on the throne of the universe, but of the Christ in the heart of the believer, " closer to us than breathing, nearer than hands and feet."

PRINCIPAL DATES

1688 Declaration of Indulgence.
1689 William and Mary.
? 16910) Nonjurors deprived.
1692 Sancroft delegates authority to Lloyd.
1694 Hickes and Wagstaffe consecrated.
1696 Fenwicke's Plot.
1702 Abjuring Oath (Anne).
1705 Dodwell's *Case in View*.
1710 Ken renounces claims. Lloyd dies.
1711 Ken dies.
1713 Collier, Spinks and Hawes consecrated.
1714 Second Abjuring Oath (George I).
1715 Jacobite Rebellion. (Hickes and Nelson die.)
1716 Hoadly attacks Nonjurors.
1718 New Service Book (Usages).
1722 Taylor consecrates two bishops for America.
1728 *Serious Call*.
1732 Instrument of Union.
1733 Campbell consecrates Laurence and Deacon for Usagers.
1741 Gordon consecrated (last in regular succession).
1745 Jacobite Rebellion.
1761 Law dies.
1805 Boothe (sole surviving bishop in either line) dies.

NONJURING EPISCOPAL SUCCESSION

The Regular Succession

1694 George Hickes.   Thomas Wagstaffe.
1713 Jeremy Collier.   Samuel Hawes.   Nathaniel Spinks.
1716 Thomas Brett, Sen.   Henry Gandy.
1721 Hilkiah Bedford.   Ralph Taylor.
1722 John Griffin.

1725   Henry Doughty.   John Blackbourne.   Henry Hall.
1727   Thomas Brett, Jun.
1728   Richard Rawlinson.   George Smith.
1731   Timothy Mawman.
1741   Robert Gordon.

The Usager Succession

1733   Roger Laurence.   Thomas Deacon.
1752   Kenrick Price.
  ?   P. J. Browne.
1780   William Cartwright.
1795   Thomas Garnett.
  ?   Charles Boothe.

BOOKS FOR FURTHER READING

HISTORIES

History of the Nonjurors. T. Lathbury. 1848.

The Nonjurors, Their Lives, Principles and Writings. J. H. Overton. 1902.

The Later Nonjurors. H. Broxap. 1924.

Social and Political Ideas of Some English Thinkers of the Augustan Age. Hearnshaw. 1928.

Church and State in England in the Eighteenth Century. Norman Sykes. 1934.

Allegiance in Church and State. L. M. Hawkins. 1928.

Also the general Church Histories including

History of the English Church from the Accession of Charles I to the Death of Anne (Ch. XIII). W. H. Hutton. 1913.

BIOGRAPHIES

Thomas Ken. F. A. Clarke. 1896.

Thomas Ken. (2 vols.) E. H. Plumptre. 1889.

Thomas Deacon. H. Broxap. 1911.

George Hickes. R. H. Collier. (Not yet published.)

Life and Opinions of William Law. J. H. Overton. 1881.

John Wesley and William Law. J. B. Green. 1945.

A Herald of the Evangelical Revival. E. W. Baker. 1948.

About William Law. A. W. Hopkinson. 1948.

William Law, A Study in Literary Craftsmanship. H. Talon. 1948.

WRITINGS EASILY ACCESSIBLE

Selected Mystical Writings of William Law. S. Hobhouse. 1948.

The Pocket William Law. A. W. Hopkinson. 1950.

Serious Call. World's Classics.

John Byrom's 'Remains.' H. Talon. 1951.

WORKS OF REFERENCE

Dictionary of National Biography.

Dictionary of English Church History. Ollard, Crosse, and Bond. 1948.